From
Gutter
to
Grace

THOMAS E. TARPLEY SR.

ISBN 978-1-64079-964-6 (Paperback)
ISBN 978-1-64079-965-3 (Digital)

Christian Faith Publishing, Inc.
296 Chestnut Street
Meadville, PA 16335
www.christianfaithpublishing.com

Printed in the United States of America

Introduction

T homas Tarpley Sr., known by most of his friends as Pastor Tom, is a retired United Methodist pastor who accepted the call of God to become an ordained pastor late in life. Throughout Tom's life, he struggled with academic learning. When he turned sixteen a few months before he was to graduate, he walked out of class one afternoon and never returned. Later, after going into the military, he obtained a General Education in Development (GED) certificate.

In 1997, at the age of fifty-five, Tom resigned from a successful career in the secular world and enrolled in the accelerated degree program at Cleary College. In a little over eleven months, he graduated with a degree in Bachelor of Science in Business Administration. Three months later, he was attending classes at the Asbury Theological Seminary in Wilmore, Kentucky, where he graduated with a Master of Divinity degree in 2001.

This publication is a written account of how a scared and timid little black boy with low self-esteem and absolutely no confidence in himself, turned to alcohol and drugs in order to cope with the challenges of life. Tom's life was plagued with emotional pain, disappointment, and failure, until one day in 1989, God spoke to him while he was on a Christian weekend retreat. After that personal encounter with Jesus, Tom surrendered his life to God and has committed his life to serving God wherever the journey may lead.

Tom, who is currently in long-term recovery from alcohol and drug abuse, has been clean and sober for over twenty-eight years, and spends his time writing and ministering to people in recovery.

From Gutter to Grace is a record of the times and trials that Tom faced in life and the events, which led him to turn from a life of sin and debauchery to a life dedicated to helping others avoid the pitfalls and the pain and suffering that filled so much of his life.

Tom's life is an incredible example of struggle, faith, and perseverance—a life that went from a person wandering around in the darkness of the wilderness to a life of spiritual joy brought on by a deep and personal relationship with Jesus.

George Mueller once said: "If any believers read this, who practically prefer other books to the Holy Scriptures, and who enjoy the writings of men much more than the word of God, may they be warned by my loss. I shall con-

4

sider this book to have been the means of doing much good, should it please the Lord, through its instrumentality, to lead some of His people no longer to neglect the Holy Scriptures, but to give them that preference, which they have hitherto bestowed on the writings of men. My dislike to increase the number of books would have been sufficient to deter me from writing these pages, had I not been convinced, that this is the only way in which the brethren at large may be benefited through my mistakes and errors, and been influenced by the hope, that in answer to my prayers, the reading of my experience may be the means of leading them to value the Scriptures more highly, and to make them the rule of all their actions."

This book is the culmination of a great deal of prayer and consultation with the Holy Spirit. A written document describing the events of my life, in an honest effort to give hope to anyone who may be experiencing some of the same hurts, hang-ups, and habits that plagued my life for far too many years.

Like Mueller states in the quote above, "It is not my desire to increase the number of books in the world," but it is my desire to try and help others who are struggling with defining their purpose in life and living up to the full potential that God has built into every living human being.

In the pages of this writing, I will share with you what it feels like to grow up feeling unloved and unwanted. I will describe how I became a master at manipulation and deception, also observations about my life of alcohol and drug abuse. I will also share with you the miracle of change that happened to me, and how I went from being a common drunk and drug abuser, to becoming a minister of the Gospel of Jesus Christ.

I am now residing in Fowlerville, Michigan, where I am still very active in spreading the Word of God and serving in Christ's church. I am the ministry leader of Celebrate Recovery and also the care pastor at the Fowlerville UB church.

It is my hope that this book will inspire whoever reads it, to look beyond their circumstances and reach out to a Holy and loving God, who is always more willing to help than we are to ask.

I begin each day with the words found in Psalm 139:23–24. "Search me, God, and know my heart; test me and know my anxious thoughts. See if there is any offensive way in me, and lead me in the way everlasting" (NIV).

Newport, Kentucky

T he most important years of a child's life are between the ages of birth to four years old. These are the years when a child develops behaviors and attitudes and learns character traits that will have an influence on his or her life for years to come.

If a child begins its life in an environment where he or she is constantly exposed to love, joy, peace, goodness, patience, kindness, gentleness, and self-control (Gal. 5:22–23), and is then shown through words and actions that he or she is loved and appreciated; when that child is given proper instructions about how to live, and receives proper corrective discipline, the child develops good behavior traits and has a very good chance of growing up into a mentally, well-developed individual who will pass those traits along to their own children.

Unfortunately for me, I did not begin my life in such an environment. My first recollections of life are filled with fear, ridicule, cruelty, intimidation, lying and deceit, no respect for the law, brutality, and hopelessness. I can remember being whipped until I started bleeding from the welts on my body, being told that I was ugly and no good, that I was just like my father, and would never amount to anything. I recall the many times of being called dumb and stupid. I remember being locked in a dark room on several occasions as punishment, because my grandma knew I was afraid of the dark. I remember scenes where my grandfather beat my grandmother with an iron poker, which was supposed to be used to stoke the fire in the big coal stove we used to heat our house. I remember seeing men and women doing things in our house that were very inappropriate for a child to see.

I still remember the night I woke up and the house was filled with policemen as they ransacked our home looking for my grandfather's illegal liquor and marijuana. I can see the handcuffs on his wrists as they led him out of the house; it was the last time I ever saw him.

I don't recall how it started, but I remember how fearful I was as a child, how I had a fear of almost everything and everyone.

For many years, I found it hard to trust anyone, because I had been deceived and let down so many times in life. Many of these things occurred before I turned five years old. Is it any wonder that I turned to alcohol and drugs to try and cope with the reality of life?

Fear was as natural to me as breathing. I can't recall a time in my life when I did not have to deal with the presence of fear. I don't know if it came from my being whipped so much as a child or from all of the negative and destructive verbal abuse I received while living with my grandmother, but whatever it was that started me to fear almost everything, it made my life a living hell.

I believe my greatest fear was putting too much emphasis on what other people thought about me. I was so afraid of making a spectacle of myself until I would always decline any opportunity to speak in front of a group or to do anything that required me to be the center of attention. As the years passed and I grew into a teenager and later into adulthood, I became more withdrawn and never allowed anyone to get too close, fearing they might see me for who I really was.

It is my hope that this book will be a source of encouragement to anyone who is living in a world dominated by fear.

Early Years

When my older brother Aaron and I were very young, our father walked out on our mother, and we moved in with my dad's parents. Mom was left to make it on her own with two young boys. With only a grade school education, it was hard for her to find work that paid enough to support us. She cleaned houses, scrubbed floors, and took in laundry; however, this was hardly enough to support our family, even in those days.

As a child living in the south with my father's parents, I never felt they loved me. I always felt like an outsider. My skin color was much darker than Aaron's whom everyone seems to be crazy about. They were always telling him what a handsome young boy he was and how good he was.

However, when it came to me, everyone ridiculed me, teased me, and called me names that were very unkind; names that made me feel inferior and lowered my self-esteem so much I didn't even like myself.

To make matters worse, I was pigeon-toed (when the toes on both feet point toward each other while walking) and clumsy; so much so, I would sometimes trip over my own feet while walking. I also stuttered when I tried to talk, (a gift I supposed was handed down from my father because he stuttered as well). I was very lonely and spent a lot of time by myself, because no one wanted to be bothered with a little black, clumsy, stuttering boy who couldn't do anything right.

When Aaron would go out to play, I tried to follow him, but he would always find a way to ditch me. I would then go back home crying and told my grandma that Aaron ran off and left me. She would tell me to shut up and go play with someone else.

Unlike the sixties, when African Americans began to take pride in their skin color and developed the slogan "Black is Beautiful," in the forties, if you were dark-skinned, you already had two strikes against you. In my case, I think I had three strikes against me, because my own family didn't want to be bothered with me.

My first years in school were terrible. I didn't enjoy being in crowds or large groups. Whenever I found myself amid people I didn't know, I always felt nervous and insecure. I didn't make friends easily and I always felt as if people were talking about me whenever I entered or left a room. My speech impairment made my life miserable.

Whenever I tried to say something, if someone laughed at me (as they most often did), I became so nervous and stuttered so badly the entire class would laugh at me, *including the teacher*. To make up for my feelings of insecurity, I became the class clown. I started to do things to disrupt the class and was always making noises like rolling a pencil back and forth on the floor with my shoe, or making funny faces behind the teacher's back to make the kids laugh. It took a long time of making a fool of myself before I realized those kids were laughing "at" me and not "with" me. By the time I reached the third grade, I spent most of the time sitting in the hallway or in the principal's office. But, for me, this was better than being in the classroom where I felt so uncomfortable. Besides, I wasn't learning anything.

I had a miserable childhood and an even worse teenage life. I learned at a very early age that alcohol would temporarily ease the pain of loneliness.

Times were tough in the South for Negroes in the forties and many of my people left to travel north to find jobs in the automobile factories in Michigan. My mother was one of those persons. She left Aaron and me with my father's parents, after my father walked out on us, then she headed north to Michigan to find work.

From what I can remember, I know my grandparents operated an illegal gambling business (otherwise known as a speakeasy) from our home.

On weekends, the house was always full of people drinking, gambling, and partying. Of course, Aaron and I were told to stay upstairs out of sight, but we would often sneak to the top of the stairs and peek down. The music and the noise were so loud we couldn't sleep anyway. Occasionally, when we thought no one was looking, we would get bold enough to run down the steps and snatch an unattended bottle of beer or a glass of moonshine and run back up the steps. Aaron and I would then drink it and act like the adults we saw downstairs.

Stealing that beer and alcohol was the beginning of what would become a life of drinking for both of us. Strangely enough, I never liked the taste of the stuff. My grandparents sold moonshine, beer, fish dinners, and a lot of other things. It was years later while living in Michigan that I realized the boxes of plants he had drying in the backyard were marijuana plants.

I remember one occasion when my grandpa was preparing for his regular weekend guests to arrive, he barbequed a whole pig. As he was carving the meat and storing it in pans, Aaron and I told him we were hungry and asked for a sandwich. He told us to go get something to eat from our grandma. He said, "This meat is for sale." I will never forget the joy I had swiping a handful of that delicious pig when he went to check on something in the house. I took it up in the hills behind our home and ate it. I was then afraid to go back in the yard where he was, because I didn't know if he had missed it. I stayed away watching from a distance until I saw him leave to go somewhere with another man before returning home. He never said anything to me so I guess he never noticed.

Aaron and I didn't get along as siblings mainly because of the difference in our ages, I suppose, but one thing I didn't realize was that when I stole the meat, Aaron had seen me. He used it to control me for a long time. Every time I would not do something he wanted me to do, he would threaten to tell on me.

My Father

I don't recall much about my father except that he was a stutterer and he was mean to my mother. The words that he finally got out of his mouth, however, we were not allowed to use. He cursed all the time, a habit I picked up and continued for most of my life.

He didn't have a good reputation around town. Some people said he was a ladies' man who would go after anything in a skirt. I know he was always getting into trouble over somebody's girlfriend or wife. I also know that he and my mother used to argue and fight a lot. He was unfaithful to my mother and moved in with another woman when he left us. Before we left Kentucky, he already had a couple of kids by the other woman.

I remember my mother telling me that one day before I was born, he was holding Aaron while she fixed dinner. As babies sometimes do, Aaron spit up on his shirt and he threw Aaron into the wood box and walked out of the room stuttering and cursing about his shirt being messed up. She said he was very particular about his appearance.

15

His shoes were always shined, his shirts had to be perfectly ironed, his trousers were always pressed, and his belt line had to be perfect.

After Mom moved up to Michigan, my father would stop by occasionally to see his parents but mostly he came to borrow money; then he was off again. If we happened to be around, he never even acknowledged that he saw us.

I remember one day seeing him climbing over the fence in the backyard; the way he kept looking back, he looked scared like someone was after him. He had been shot, and blood was all over his shirt. Going to the hospital was out of the question, so my grandma (who evidently had performed this feat in the past for him) patched him up (he was always getting into trouble).

When he left that day, it was the last time I saw or heard anything about him until the day someone called my mother several years later in Michigan to inform her that he had passed away from complications brought on by tuberculosis.

My dad and my mother had never gotten a divorce, so she was still listed as his spouse. My mother wasn't home when the call came in, so I answered the call, but I forgot to tell my mother until she asked me about it several weeks or months later. I must have been around the age of fourteen or fifteen, but once I hung up the phone, and went outside to play, it never entered my mind again until she asked me about it.

My brother hated my dad because he walked out on us, but I have never held anything against my dad because I never knew him. All I know about him is what other people told me. In a way, when people would say I was just like him, it made me feel good because then, I had somebody with whom I could identify.

We never heard anything else from the person who called or anyone else from my dad's side of the family.

Grandma

A couple of years after I was born, my dad left my mother and moved in with another woman. Unable to find work, Mom decided to move north to Michigan, where Mom's younger sister lived with her family.

Mom had heard that jobs were plentiful for women (especially in the factories). Because it was during the war, a lot of the young men were overseas fighting for our country, and the factories in Pontiac were hiring lots of women to do the jobs that the men used to do.

Leaving us in the care of our father's parents was not Mom's first choice; but at the time, it was the best she could do. When Mom made up her mind to go to Michigan, she couldn't afford to take us with her. Although she would stay with her sister for a while, she didn't know where she was going to live or how long it would take her to find employment. Both of Mom's parents were deceased, and none of her other relatives were willing to take on the responsibility of caring for two young children.

My brother Aaron and I found out very soon after she left that our grandparents were not very nice people; they treated us more like indentured servants rather than grandchildren.

I was still a toddler when Mom left, so I had it easy. Aaron, however, who was almost five years older than I, had it rough: Grandma always had him doing something around the house. He still found time, however, to get into mischief: like making a batch of homemade corncob wine one summer. He learned how to do this by watching my grandpa make wine and moonshine.

Aaron stole sugar from the kitchen and hid it in a lard bucket until he had enough to make the wine (about fifteen pounds of sugar). Then he took the leftover corncobs from one of the weekend parties and added water and the stolen sugar and filled the bucket with water. He let it age until it was ready. We had a place up in the hills behind our house where we used to go and hide when we didn't want to be found. If Grandma called us, we pretended we didn't hear her. Of course, we got yelled at when we finally did show up but we got used to that. Grandma was always yelling about something.

I can't remember exactly how old I was when I got drunk on that homemade wine; I do remember that it was before I entered elementary school. The wine was very sweet and I didn't like it, but I knew I was doing something that I should not have been doing and that made me want to continue. There has always been something about breaking the rules that excited me. Aaron and I drank until we started to feel a little woozy; but instead of stopping, I continued to drink. After gulping down several cups of that homemade concoction, I tried to stand up, but I fell. My head was spinning so fast I became sick and began to empty my stomach. At this point, I think Aaron was okay because he didn't drink as much as I did. He kept telling me I had better stop, but I didn't listen to him.

All it took to get me started was one drink, after that, I became powerless and lost control over how much I drank. The other major problem is: I never like to merely sip anything I drink; I always just gulp it down. I still don't like the taste of the stuff. But the warm fuzzy feeling I get after taking the first drink triggers an uncontrollable urge to take more. Maybe if I had drunk at a slower pace, I could have felt the effects of it sooner and quit before I got too sick.

All the details as to what happened that day are not quite as clear as they were a few years ago. I do recall Aaron was scared out of his wits because he thought our grandmother would find out—then we would be in big trouble. After throwing up several more times, Aaron kept me away from the house until I could walk; then he slipped me up to our room where I immediately fell asleep. I slept a very long time and woke up feeling sick.

A normal person, with half a brain (who got as sick as I did and felt as bad as I felt), would have realized that drinking was not a good thing to do and would not have touched it again! But not me! The next day, I went back up in the hills behind the house and started all over again.

Guess what? The same thing happened; it was to be like that for the next forty-three years. I had absolutely no control over how much I drank once I started. One drink was always one too many; a case full was never enough. I have come to understand that I have an addictive personality and abuse almost anything I enjoy doing.

I often wondered why my grandma never caught on to what we were doing, but I guess it was because she and my grandpa drank all the time so they couldn't smell it on us.

It is a good thing we never got caught because our grandma was a strict disciplinarian who didn't believe in sparing the rod and spoiling the child. She used to whip us with ironing cords, razor straps, or weeping willow switches braided together. She left welts on us that didn't go down for days.

In those days, Child Protective Services didn't exist, at least not as far as we were concerned. More than once, she beat us until we bled from where the ironing cord or razor strap tore into our skins.

Because of Grandma's size (I have been told that she weighed over 300 lbs.), whipping me was not an easy task.

I would scream even before she hit me; then I would run and crawl under the bed or some other piece of furniture. Because I was small and agile, I could easily outmaneuver her. When I would dive under the bed, she would go get a broom or something to poke at me, and while she was gone, I would run and hide or at least try to hide. When she caught up with me, I would grab the belt or switch and hold on. Sometimes, the switch would break (or I would tear it apart), forcing her to get another. I would kick and scream, and wrap myself around her legs like a human pretzel. I begged and pleaded and promised never to be bad again. I hollered like she was killing me—even before she ever touched me. Sometimes, she would get tired and give up because struggling and wrestling with me caused her to wheeze and cough; she would leave me alone with the promise that "she would get me later;" she always kept her promise.

She would wait until I went to sleep, then sneak into my room and tie my feet together so I couldn't run. I have always been a very sound sleeper. She would grab hold of one of my hands and proceed to beat the living daylights out of me; I would wake up in the middle of the night feeling the aftermath of the sting of the belt or switch.

The thing I never understood was when she hit me and I screamed she would yell at me to shut up and then hit me again. Naturally, I screamed again, and she kept saying shut up! And all the while she's whipping me, she's telling me about each thing I did that led up to the punishment I was receiving.

Aaron didn't give her as much trouble as I did. Whenever he got a whipping, he would stand there and take it, and he wouldn't even cry. Grandma would hit him three or four times. When she saw she was not going to make him cry, she would leave him alone.

However, one day, when he was getting ready to wash some of our socks, Aaron had boiled a kettle full of water. He was just about to pour the boiling water into the pan on the socks when I told him I didn't want him to wash mine so he told me to take them out.

When I stuck my hand into the pan to retrieve my socks, he poured the scalding hot water on my arm. I was burned so badly you could see the bone in my arm. I screamed, and Grandma came into the room to see what had happened. You might say he burned the pee out of me because when that scalding hot water hit me, I emptied my bladder right there in the middle of the floor.

When she saw Aaron standing there with the kettle of boiling water, after she had looked at my badly injured arm, she grabbed an ironing cord and began to beat him like she was trying to kill him. She hit him everywhere she could—on the back, legs, head, even across the face. This was the first time he didn't stand still and take it; he tried to dodge the blows and even grabbed the cord and held on to it so he could stop her from hitting him.

Meanwhile, I'm screaming and running around trying to get her to help me, but she didn't pay me any attention until she finished with him. Afterwards, I actually felt sorry for him because she had beat him so bad, he looked worse than I did. He had welts all over his body and face. She kept him in the house until most of the swelling had gone down. After treating my arm with an old folk remedy, she took me out and bought me some ice cream. It was the first time I ever felt like she had some feeling for me. The feeling didn't last long, because in the next few days as my arm started to heal, she was her old ridiculing self again.

She would tease me about being clumsy and how ashy my skin became after she gave me a bath (I have always had very dry skin). In those days, lotion was out of the question, she would simply scoop out a handful of lard and grease me down like a pig for a greased pig race. I hated when she did that, because she made me wear wool trousers and I could not stand to have the material next to my skin. When she greased me up like a pig, I was even more miserable. Sometimes, I would slip up to my room and put my pajamas on underneath my clothes to ease the discomfort.

I don't have any good memories of my time with my grandmother. I never heard anything about her after we left her home until one year after we were grown, Aaron looked her up and went to see her. He spent a few days with her and one of our half brothers. My dad had some more children after we left Kentucky, but I never knew them.

When Aaron came back, he told me that Grandma wanted to see me, but I never went down. The next time I heard from them was after she passed away, my younger half brother called, looking for money to bury her. It angered me that they had never thought about contacting me until they needed something. I placed the receiver down and closed that chapter of my life.

Mom to the Rescue

After I turned five and started school, our mother came down from Michigan to visit us. She told Grandma she would soon be able to take us up north with her. Grandma told Mom she was not going to give us up.

I believe one of Grandma's reasons was that she had gotten used to having us around, and she didn't want to part with us. She needed someone to run errands and to do a lot of the physical things she was not able to do. Since my grandfather was still in jail, we were all she had. She kept us busy cleaning and doing what she should have been doing, had she been able to bend over.

It may sound as if I have a lot of resentment for my grandma, but quite the contrary. I was so naïve and stupid until I liked her and tried to get her to like me. I didn't realize how mean she was and how we were simply being used to make her life easier. I'm not sure but I think she may have been getting money from the government to take care of us.

After several heated arguments with my grandmother, Mom soon left and returned to Michigan (but not without a plan). Mom and Aaron had gotten their heads together while she was visiting. She had given him instructions on what to do when she was ready to come and get us. (Naturally, none of this was revealed to me because I was a tattletale and would have told my grandma.)

Mom's plan was to intercept us one day on our way to school; she was determined to get us away from our grandma. Financially, she was not able to do so at the time of her visit because if she took us north with her, she would have to pay for child care while she worked, which she could not afford.

Mom was patient. When the opportunity presented itself for her to get into one of the automobile plants, she quickly took advantage of the increased income and had high hopes of bringing us home to be with her.

However, that job didn't last long because the war ended. When the troops began to return home, the women were laid off to make room for the men. Mom went back to doing day work (cleaning white folks' houses), sometimes working two jobs. She was trying to save enough money so she could return to Kentucky and get us away from our grandmother. Aaron used to sneak and write letters to her (unknown to me) telling her how badly we were being treated.

When Mom finally got things in order, and was ready to come get us, Grandma kept her word and refused to let us go. So, Mom and Aaron put their plan into action: whereby we would leave for school one day, and meet Mom at the bus stop. She would then take us to our aunt's home, who lived in Murfreesboro, Tennessee; my grandma would never have thought to look for us there. Of course, I didn't know about the plan. Nobody tells a tattletale anything.

The plan was for us to stay with our aunt until the heat was off. The plan worked and we were taken down to my aunt Mary and uncle Fred's home in Murfreesboro, Tennessee, where we stayed for almost three years.

When Grandma discovered what Mom had done, she was red hot. She tried to find us and even threatened my mother with legal action, but soon gave up because Grandma did not have legal custody of us. There was nothing Grandma could do.

In case you're wondering about my grandpa's part in all this, I can't actually say, but I believe he was in prison at the time. We (Aaron and I) never heard anything about him after the night the police took him away in handcuffs.

One thing Mom did not count on, nor did any of us know at the time, was that I had a nervous stomach. I had never been in a car to go any real distance, so we didn't know that riding in an automobile made me sick to my stomach. The bus driver wasn't too happy about it either;

he had to pull over and fling open the door every time Mom yelled out, "Stop the bus!" I think we were fortunate to have a bus driver with a compassionate heart.

In those days, he could have easily left us by the side of the road and nothing would have been said about it. After what seemed like an eternity, we arrived at the bus station in Tennessee, where Uncle Fred and one of his friends met us. Uncle Fred's friend drove us out to our uncle and aunt's place. (Uncle Fred didn't own a car; good thing too, he didn't know how to drive).

Mom didn't go out to our aunt's home with us. She hugged us and kissed us and told us that we were to go stay with our aunt and be good little boys until she came to get us. She turned, walked over to the ticket window, and purchased a one-way ticket to Pontiac. I could see the tears in her eyes as she waved good-bye as Uncle Fred led us toward the car. It would be almost three years before we would see her again. She did write us on a regular basis, and we always received a package on our birthdays and around Christmas time.

One year, she sent me the neatest pair of cap pistols I had ever seen, and she sent Aaron a Red Ryder BB gun. (I don't know what Mom was thinking about on that one.) Aaron and one of our cousins who lived in the next town were over to our cousin's house playing one day. The man who lived behind our cousin raised pigs. We were sitting around on the porch when suddenly the pig owner came around the corner of the house screaming at my brother and cousin. He claimed they had crippled one of his pigs. The man said he found BB's in one of the pig's legs and that he had seen my brother actually shoot the pig.

My brother lost possession of his BB gun for a few days and both the boys got a brushing. Whenever my cousin's father would give them a spanking, he called it a brushing because he used a big wide hair brush to paddle them. It was kind of enjoyable to watch Aaron and my cousin get spanked. Usually, it was me on the receiving end of the paddle.

Life in Murfreesboro

L iving with Aunt Mary and Uncle Fred and their two daughters, (who were teenagers), was a real change from those first years with my grandparents. Aaron and I didn't know it at the time, but we were in for a whole new way of life. It wouldn't be too hard getting used to being talked to (instead of being yelled at), being asked to do something (instead of being told what to do), and being able to go out and play with our friends; all the while not having to worry about being called in to perform some menial task, like holding the dustpan for my grandma while she swept the trash into it because she was too big to bend overs.

Aunt Mary acted like she was happy to see us because she kept hugging and kissing us. One of the first differences we noticed upon our arrival was there was no bathroom in the house. When we asked about it, Uncle Fred took us outside and showed us this little wooden shed—just big enough to step into and turn around. It smelled like nothing I had ever smelled before. He told us this was the out-

THOMAS E. TARPLEY SR.

house where we went when we had to use the bathroom. It didn't look like the bathroom at my grandmother's; it was merely a hole in the ground with a box over it with a hole cut in the top for a seat. There was a department store catalog hanging on the wall; I thought it was for looking at the pictures. That little shed was moved several times before we left to go to Michigan.

Then Uncle Fred took us over to a water pump with a bucket hanging on the handle. He told us one of our duties would be to make sure Aunt Mary had enough water in the house at all times; and that this task was to be one of our daily chores. Aaron and I had never laid eyes on a pump before so we looked at each other like a couple of deer caught in the headlights while standing in the middle of the road—motionless.

Grandma may have been mean and treated us badly, but at least she had electricity and indoor plumbing.

We began to wonder if our mother loved us; after all, she had just dropped us off with two people we had never seen before who had no indoor plumbing and no electricity in the house. Light was provided by several oil lanterns, and the big iron-looking monster in the corner of the kitchen served as a cooking stove as well as to heat the house in the winter.

For entertainment, they had this long radio connected to a battery of the same size. We used to sit around it on

Saturday night listening to the *Grand Old Opry* while I tried to figure out how so many people got into that tiny little box.

The next change we encountered was church. Aunt Mary and Uncle Fred were devout Christians who belonged to a full-gospel, foot-stomping, hand-clapping, get-up-off-your-butt, get happy, and "get your shout on" church.

I remember a sermon the pastor preached one Sunday; one which had a lasting effect on me. It was a fire and brimstone sermon that talked about how sinners would burn in hell forever and ever. This sermon had a lot to do with me eventually turning my life over to Christ. It put the fear of God in me.

Before going to Aunt Mary's, Aaron and I had never been in a church before. The only time we had ever seen a pastor was when my grandma's sister and brother passed away on two different occasions. This new experience with church people was quite different from the kind of people to which we had been exposed in Kentucky.

The first Sunday after we got there, Uncle Fred woke us up and announced that it was time to get up and get ready for church. Something Aunt Mary was cooking smelled delicious so Aaron and I hurried outside to the pump to wash up in the washing pan that was hung by the side of the pump. Uncle Fred was already dressed; he had been up for hours. He told us that if we got up early enough the next Sunday, we could watch him wring the neck off a chicken.

Having someone fix breakfast for us was new; we only had a bowl of cold cereal and milk when we lived with our grandma. Sometimes when there was no milk, we ate it with water. After washing up, we went back inside to find my aunt putting the meal on the table. She had prepared a full dinner meal with biscuits, gravy, mashed potatoes, fried chicken, and vegetables; we had never seen a meal like this before, not even at dinner time. After tasting it, we discovered that Aunt Mary was a very good cook.

We thought she did this especially for us, but we found out that this was their Sunday tradition. On Sunday morning, Uncle Fred would get up early, wash up, and get dressed. He would then go out and catch one of the chickens that were free-roaming around the yard. He would hold onto the head, and, with a quick motion of the wrist, he would twirl it around until all he was holding was the head. Meanwhile, the rest of the chicken was flopping all over the yard. Watching him do that one time was enough for me. Like I said earlier, I have a nervous stomach.

Sunday mornings when we left home for church, we sometimes didn't return until late in the day. On those Sunday's when she knew it was going to be close to dark when we got back, we had dinner in the morning before we left.

The next surprise was neither my uncle nor my aunt drank alcohol. They believed it was a sin to drink alcohol of any kind. For the next three years, Aaron and I would not have a single drink of anything except milk, lemonade, or water.

We had to go over to the neighbor's farm to get the milk right out of the cow. Uncle Fred loaded a large metal container in a wagon; then we would walk to the neighbor's farm. Uncle Fred would pay him and then Uncle Fred would sit down on a stool and milk the cow himself. One day, he let me try my hand at milking. I spilled some milk on the ground. Within a few minutes, there were all kinds of creatures moving around in it. I still don't drink milk to this day.

As time went by, we became accustomed to our new environment. Uncle Fred, who was a quiet, mild-mannered man, worked with me to help me overcome my stuttering. He told me that when I started to stutter, to simply stop and start over; before I left Tennessee, I was able to get out a whole sentence before I started to stutter.

As usual, boys will be boys—and we found ways of getting into trouble. After we had been with our aunt for almost three years, we pulled off a stunt that frightened Aunt Mary to a point where she decided it was time for Aaron and me to return to our mother.

THOMAS E. TARPLEY SR.

Uncle Fred owned a little black-and-white terrier named Tiny. Tiny was not vicious and he loved to play. We kept him on a long chain connected to the woodshed. One day, we heard him barking and saw him running around trying to get at something in the bushes behind the woodshed.

Aaron and I knew what was causing Tiny to act the way he was, because this was not the first time it had happened. A little white boy who lived in the neighborhood would come over to the vacant field where there was a huge pile of rocks. It was an abandoned factory site used to store gravel, rocks and other building supplies. The boy would hide in the bushes, and then throw rocks at Tiny. Tiny would do his best to get free of his chain; he would strain and bark, and jump up and down trying to free himself.

Aaron and I decided it was time to teach the boy a lesson. We unhooked Tiny and let him go; Tiny was fast and he could run like greased lightning! In a few seconds, we heard a loud scream. We ran up on a hill so we could see over the bushes. We could see the boy running away with Tiny snapping at his rear end as he went. Aaron, who had trained Tiny to come when he whistled, whistled for Tiny, and, fortunately, he came back. We locked him in the woodshed and then worked on the story we would tell if the boy went home and told his parents.

He did. We didn't need a crystal ball to tell us that we were in trouble. In those days, especially in the south, the last thing you wanted to do (if you were a Negro) was to get on the wrong side of a white person.

We decided to make it look as if Tiny broke free from his chain on his own. We took a pair of pliers and separated the chain in half by pulling one of the links apart. We attached part of the broken chain to his collar. The other part we left chained to the building; then we locked Tiny back in the woodshed. A short time later, two of the biggest policemen (both white) I had ever seen came walking down the hill toward our house. Aaron and I looked at each other as if to say, "Oh, boy, we're in for it now!"

Before I share with you what happened with the policemen, I want to tell you a little about what it was like growing up as a black person in the south.

If you were a Negro, which black people were called then, you did not talk back to a white man or white woman: You say "yes, sir" and "yes, ma'am" when addressing either. You never looked white folk straight in the eye; you usually kept your head down, so as not to make eye contact. If you were told to do something by a white person, you did it without question.

One of the worst things you could do (as a Negro) was to smile, touch, or hug a white female. (It didn't matter how ugly or homely she was).

In some counties, south, of where we lived, young Negro boys who violated this unwritten and unspoken "code" came up missing and were never found.

Until we moved to Tennessee, the only white people we encountered were the policemen who occasionally visited our house unannounced, seeking to catch my grandfather in some illegal activity.

But things were different in Tennessee. All of our neighbors were white, and they all worked for the railroad. They lived in row homes built by the railroad company; each morning, you could see the men walking down the hill to catch a flat car as the train passed by. It came by every morning, moving slowly enough for the men to jump on board; in the evening, it would return them home the same way.

Uncle Fred was one of the few black men in the crew. Because Uncle Fred was a man of integrity and well-respected in the community, most of the people overlooked some of the mischief Aaron and I used to get into. Believe me, we got into a lot!

Almost all the black people we met were afraid to speak up to white people. Aaron and I got bopped in the mouth more than once for expressing our mind to a white person. Aunt Mary would say things like, "You keep quiet, you don't talk to white people that way." When I would try to explain my side of it, I got bopped again.

Aaron was very strong-willed; he was not used to behaving meekly. He did everything he could to show people he was not afraid to speak his mind. My aunt and uncle put up with us, but after a while, we could tell they were getting tired of us.

The day the police showed up was the straw that broke the camel's back. Aunt Mary was so afraid that she and Uncle Fred were going to be arrested or worse, she began trembling in fear.

When the officers arrived, the parents of the little boy (who had been bitten) were present. The boy's parents were angry, and wanted the police to arrest all of us and to have Tiny shot. The boy was with them too, but he wouldn't come in the yard.

Thank God Uncle Fred had a good reputation in the community and was well-known for his honesty and integrity. Almost everyone liked him. The officers questioned him first, then they had him call us over so they could ask us what happened.

We shared with them how the boy would come every day, and throw rocks at Tiny; and how sometimes, when a stone hit him, Tiny would go crazy, and try to break free from his chain. We told them Tiny must have broken free, and gone after the boy. We even showed them the chain, and all the rocks lying around where Tiny had been chained up.

Lying through our teeth, we told them we were not around when it happened, but when we came back and saw Tiny free of his chain, we locked him in the woodshed.

The policemen told us we could go; then, they talked with Uncle Fred some more. To our surprise, they all left, the parents with their son, and the police together. It was plain to see that the parents were not happy, as they were still fussing. As they walked away, I heard one of the officers tell them they needed to keep their son away from our place.

That night, we heard Aunt Mary tell Uncle Fred that it was time for us to go. She said, "If they stay here, they're going to get us killed. I'm writing their mother tomorrow, and tell her if she doesn't come and get them, we're going to put them in a home." We were being uprooted again, but this time, it was good because we were going to be with Mom. Grandma had given up, long ago, of ever getting us back so there was nothing to fear from her.

It wasn't long after that when Aunt Mary received a letter from Mom telling her that she was sending Mrs. Pruitt, a friend of Mom's, to bring us home. Mom was unable to come herself because she was expecting a baby. Mrs. Pruitt showed up about a week later. She spent the night with us. The next day, we headed off with her to the bus station where we would catch a bus to Michigan to be reunited with our mother. We would never again be separated for the rest of her life.

The thought of being moved again was terrifying. It had taken me a long time to adjust to our new environment in Tennessee and, now that I was feeling comfortable with my new surroundings, we were being moved again. I had already started to think about the new neighborhood and what the kids were like. I wondered if I would be able to make friends and how I would fit in, what my mom's new boyfriend was like, would he like us, etc. My mind invented all kinds of problems and that old familiar fear of the unknown began to creep up on me once again.

Oh No! Not Another Bus

I f you will recall, my trip south from Kentucky to Tennessee was not a pleasant journey. The trip north to Michigan was much worse because it was several hundred miles longer than the trip from Kentucky to Tennessee.

By the time we arrived in Michigan, we had been asked to leave one bus, and Mrs. Pruitt had almost been arrested.

My motion sickness was a real problem; and I remember that the other people on the buses looked at me like I had leprosy. A couple of times when one of the bus drivers didn't stop fast enough, I let go right there—all over the seat—and anybody who was close to me. The bus driver told Mrs. Pruitt, our traveling companion, that if it happened again we would have to leave the bus.

Mrs. Pruitt was a northern woman and a very proud woman, at that. She let the bus driver know (in words that we were not allowed to use) just how she felt about the situation. She told him she had paid her fare, and we would not be getting off until we reached our destination.

About a few more miles down the road, I felt my stomach churning again, feeling like it was going to erupt—which it did. It happened so fast, I didn't have time to make it to the door before I sprayed the whole right side of the bus. The bus driver was furious! He stopped the bus and told us to get off.

After a long and heated conversation between the bus driver and Mrs. Pruitt, the bus driver agreed to take us to the next rest stop, but then we would have to change buses. Aaron seemed to be enjoying the confrontation between Mrs. Pruitt and the bus driver because she didn't kowtow or look intimidated when he spoke to her.

Neither one of us had ever seen a black person talk to a white person the way Mrs. Pruitt talked to that white bus driver. I think he may have been a little afraid of her because she was not a small woman. She spoke with pride and dignity, not like other Negroes we had heard talk to white people.

We were sure we were going to be arrested or lynched. At the next stop, we gathered up our luggage, got off the bus, and followed the other passengers to a restaurant to get something to eat.

We noticed that the other Negroes on the bus didn't follow us; they went in another direction. When we got to the restaurant, we found out why. There were signs on the door and plastered all over the windows, which read, "We don't serve colored."

As we were standing there, the bus driver came up and told us that there was a place down the street that served our kind, and we could catch another bus going north, in about two hours. He handed Mrs. Pruitt three slips of paper, which I later learned were transfer slips, then he turned and went to find a bucket and some water to clean up his bus.

Sure enough, there was a small shack that looked like it should have been condemned several years ago. There was a sign in the window, "Colored folks welcome here." We went inside and almost opted out of eating because the place was not in the best condition; flies were all over the place and it smelled *awful!* Mrs. Pruitt just shook her head, walked up to the counter, and asked what could we get to go. After paying for our order, we took it outside and sat on a bench beside the restaurant and ate our meal.

After eating, and finally transferring to another bus, we ran into another problem. We were still in the south; in those days, Negroes were not allowed to sit in the front of the bus. As it turned out, there were only two seats in the rear of the bus, so Aaron and I took them. After looking around for another seat, Mrs. Pruitt spotted a seat up near the front. She proudly moved down the aisle, and plopped right down beside a white woman. The woman yelled to

the bus driver, "Bus driver, would you please tell this n—
that she can't sit here!" The bus driver told Mrs. Pruitt
that she would have to get up, and move to the back. Mrs.
Pruitt said, "Fine, you find me a seat back there and I'll
gladly move to it." Then she proceeded to tell the woman
who called her a n— what she (Mrs. P.) thought about
her. She must have made an impression on her because the
white woman turned a deep crimson red and never opened
her mouth for the rest of the trip as far as I know.

Now, every eye on the bus was on Mrs. Pruitt and the
bus driver, waiting to see what was going to happen next.

He stopped the bus, got up out of his seat, and walked
up and down the aisle. There was not one seat available in
the rear of the bus. Some of the seats in the back were occupied by whites, but he didn't ask any of them to change
with Mrs. Pruitt.

He came back to Mrs. Pruitt and said, "I'm sorry, there
are no seats in the rear, but you cannot sit here." Mrs. Pruitt
had a very light complexion; Aaron and I could see her
turning a deep shade of red or purple, veins were popping
out of her temple, and as she stood up, she put her hands
on both hips, and looked the bus driver straight in the eye.
She said, "I paid my fare to Pontiac, Michigan. That is
where I expect you to take me. And I don't intend to stand
up all the way there." Then she sat back down.

The bus driver leaned over, and said something to the white lady sitting next to her. Then he returned to his seat and started the bus. Boy, this Mrs. Pruitt was a bad woman. We were just hoping she didn't get us all lynched.

A few miles down the road, Aaron yelled for the bus driver to pull over, to allow me to get rid of my lunch. When I finished, he called me up front, and opened a large box beside his seat. He took out several brown bags. He said, "The next time you feel like you're going to throw up, stick your head in the bag." I thought, *Why didn't the other bus drivers think of this?*

After several more rest stops, another change of buses, and for what seemed like an eternity, we finally arrived at the bus depot in Pontiac, Michigan.

That was the summer of 1950. Mrs. Pruitt took us to her home where my mother was living with her boyfriend in an upstairs apartment. When we saw our mother, we were so happy, we hugged her while she cried.

I was happy for one of the first times in my life. I had just turned eight years old; and Aaron was almost thirteen. For most of our young lives, we only had seen Mom for a few days at a time when she would come and visit us. Now we were with her to stay; this was a happy day in our lives.

Shortly after we arrived, Mrs. Pruitt took Aaron and my mom downtown, but they made me stay at home because she was afraid I would get sick in the cab. I sat on the front steps until they returned, feeling that old sense of loneliness that I had become so familiar with whenever I was abandoned and left to myself.

18 Beaudette Street

In January of 1951, my little sister Rebecca was born. Mom was not married to her father and later they decided to go their separate ways.

Soon after, Mom started keeping company with a very nice man named Gus, whom I liked. He owned his own home and operated a very lucrative business out of his home. After about a year of dating Gus, he and Mom decided that they wanted to live together, so we moved into Gus's home. Our new address was Eighteen Beaudette Street, where I would live until I was eighteen years old.

In those days, a lot of Negroes chose to live by what is known as "Common Law Marriage." They moved in together, and set up housekeeping, living as husband and wife. Although Mom and Gus never got legally married, he loved her deeply, and treated her with caring respect. He treated us as though we were his own children. At last I had a family: Mom, Gus, (whom I later began to call "Dad"), Aaron, Rebecca, and me. Five and six years later, two more siblings were added to our family, a sister and a brother.

Pontiac was unlike any place in which I had ever lived. The streets were all paved, almost everyone had automobiles. Everyone, except us, that is. Gus had never learned to drive, and, even though he could pay cash for any car he wanted, he had never owned one. He used to walk everywhere he went.

We could go to the movies and sit anywhere we liked. Negroes and whites went to school together; we could go into any business downtown and get served just like the white people. I knew I was going to like living in Michigan.

My new dad didn't drink, but he kept several fifths of liquor in the back of his closet, which he only brought out for special occasions—like spiking eggnog on Thanksgiving and Christmas. All his liquor had been gifts from others around Christmas time for favors he had done for them. My new dad was in business for himself as one of the most respected and trusted Street Numbers men in town. He was honest and you never had to worry about being cheated out of your winnings if your number came in.

On our first Thanksgiving together, we gathered around the table for the delicious meal Mom had prepared. We had company from Detroit, some of Dad's relatives, two of which were young pretty girls. Dad, who always gave God thanks before every meal, insisted that we eat our meals together as a family. Dad was not a religious person, and never attended church; but he believed in God and lived by the golden rule. He treated everyone fairly and would share anything he had with anyone in need.

When it came time for dessert, he pulled out a fifth of expensive bourbon and poured some into all our glasses; then he filled them with eggnog. That was a big mistake: this was the first time I had tasted alcohol since leaving Kentucky.

I had almost forgotten those early years of drinking when I lived in Kentucky. When I tasted the alcohol in my eggnog and felt the warmness of the liquor, I knew I was going to visit the back of Dad's closet the next time he left home.

It started with stealing drinks from my stepdad's closet, then growing into an out-of-control habit and lifestyle of drinking that would plague me for many years to come.

Before I leave this chapter, I want to share something about Gus, the man who became my dad. I never saw him enter a church. I never heard him say he was a Christian, but everything about him made him stand a cut above anybody else I have ever met. He was a man of great wisdom and well-versed on almost any subject. Gus was as humble as anyone I've ever known, and his honesty and integrity were beyond reproach.

Gus knew the scriptures as well or better than anyone I have ever met. If you wanted to discuss the Bible with him, you had better come armed with knowledge and powered by the Holy Spirit because he not only knew the Bible, he lived it.

About two years after we moved in with him, his sister contacted him and asked him to help her. She was about to lose her car and asked him to take over the payments. Gus agreed to do it, so she signed the car over to him; he paid it off the next week. He didn't like credit, usually paying cash for everything he bought.

As I said earlier, Gus never learned to drive, so the car just sat in our yard for several weeks. One day Gus got up, went out to the car and started to read the owner's manual.

A couple of days later, he started the car, and began to back up and then pull forward (we had a long, wide driveway). He did this for several days, until he felt comfortable behind the wheel.

A few days after practicing in the driveway, he walked down to the police station and picked up a copy of the Handbook for Michigan Drivers. Two days after studying the book, he went down and took his driver's license exam. He passed. He took the road test, which he also passed. He had taught himself to drive right there in our driveway and then read the handbook on licensing; he took the test and obtained his license. He drove the car for a few months after that but one day, he came home with a brand new vehicle.

The day he arrived home with the new vehicle, he was a little hot under the collar because the first dealer he went to wouldn't sell it to him; Gus had no credit history. That really ticked Gus off; so he walked out of the dealership, went to another dealer down the street, and purchased a brand new Ford for cash.

Then he asked the salesman, who sold him the car, to call down the street to the other dealer, and tell the first dealer's salesman that he just sold a car for cash to the man who had just been in his showroom and was turned away.

Gus always hated it when someone told him he couldn't do something. After that, anytime he made a big purchase, he would pay half up front; then a couple of weeks later, he would pay it off. This enabled him to establish a credit history, and avoid being rejected when he tried to buy something on terms.

He told me the only reason he wanted credit was to make sure that what he bought was free of defects. If he paid half, and had no problems with the purchase, he would pay it off. If something was wrong with it, or it had a defect, he would hold off making the final payment until the seller made it right.

The Hood

We lived in a neighborhood that had lots of kids. On my side of the street, in my block, there were only four houses; three of which were three-story with an apartment on each floor. The fourth was a two-story, four-family flat. In those four houses, there were at least twelve different families. Two of those families had ten children and one family had eight. In my house, there were only seven kids. The people on the third floor had two children and there were five of us in our family. The second floor was occupied by a single, elderly woman who rented out one of her rooms to a single, elderly man. The house next door to us had a family on each floor, and even had a family living in the basement.

When you add the single family homes on the other side of the street (about five), there were approximately fifty to sixty kids living in the block where I grew up.

In all, including the families across the street, one of which had eight children, there were over seventy kids of all ages living on our street.

Naturally, being the new kids on the block, and only the two of us to boot, some of the other kids tried to bully us by pushing us around.

Aaron earned his place in the community early. One late afternoon, as we were walking home from the movies, one of the boys on the block came running by and splashed water on my brother's pants. The boy's name was Mark. Aaron yelled an obscenity at him. Mark stopped, turned around, came, and got right up in Aaron's face. Aaron didn't flinch, but stood his ground. Mark asked my brother to repeat what he said, and Aaron quickly repeated it with a few more cuss words that made Mark even more angry. Mark told my brother that he would kick his butt if Aaron didn't take back what he said. Aaron told him to go ahead and try; the only thing between them was air and opportunity. The next thing I knew, they were rolling on the ground, punching each other. Mark realized that he was not going to be able to get the best of Aaron, so he broke free, stood up, and said, "I'm going to get my brother, he'll take care of you." Aaron said, "Go get him, I'm not stopping you."

Mark ran a few houses down and went into his house, which was right down the street. Through the large picture window, we could see a lot of boys and men of all ages walking around inside. We decided we had better move on before he and his brothers came back and kicked our butts.

So we took off running. (By the way I was a pretty fast runner because I was always running from somebody who wanted to pummel my head in the ground.)

After that, word got around that one of the new kids was no pushover; Aaron didn't have any further problems fitting in with the other boys his age. Later on, he even had a brief courtship with Mark's older sister. Soon after that, Mark and I began to hang out together, and he became one of my closest friends.

It didn't take long for me to develop a reputation for being a bad little boy who was always in trouble. When the school year started, I was in the third grade. I spent more time in the hallway sitting outside of my class than I did in the classroom. I was always acting out to hide my insecurities.

The teacher was always sending me to the principal's office. Occasionally, they sent a note home to my mother, which always seemed to get lost on the way home.

It was only a matter of months before the other kids' mothers started to give me the "evil eye," whenever I came around; some parents even forbade their children to play with me. They said I was a bad influence.

Most of the kids my age avoided me because they thought I was silly, and no fun to be around. I would usually hang out with kids who were younger than me or around older kids who would let me tag along as long as I had some money to spend. I used to steal money from my mom's purse or from my brother's pants pocket at night after he went to bed. Aaron had gotten a paper route a few months after we arrived in town; his pockets were always full of change. I used the money to buy candy and then give it to the older kids so they would let me hang out with them. As soon as I ran out of money or candy, they usually ditched me. For the most part, I spent a lot of time alone, because I felt uncomfortable around kids my own age who usually liked to play softball, skate, and do other things most boys did. Nobody wanted me on their team, because I was not good at anything! When teams were choosing up sides, I was the last one to be chosen for a team, if I got chosen at all.

I began smoking at the age of nine, because I thought it made me look cool. I learned how to curse, and to swear like a pro. I thought the more curse words I used, the more it made me fit in with the older boys.

My mouth was filthy; I thought I was making an impression on the older kids. I liked the looks of the Viceroy Cigarette pack, so that was what I smoked. Cigarettes were no problem for me to get. I was so skinny, I could stick my arm up in the slot on the cigarette vending machines, curl the tip of my double-jointed finger into a hook, and flip out pack after pack of cigarettes.

In the early 1950s, cigarettes were twenty-two cents per pack. There were three pennies taped to the pack (inside the cellophane wrapper); which was the change from the quarter you had to put into machine. I would take the pennies off the pack and then sell the cigarettes I didn't want. In those days, ten cents could get you an awful lot of candy.

Before I went into the house, I would always hide my cigarettes under the porch, because Mom and Dad would have been on my case if they knew what I was doing. I learned early how to be very sneaky and became a very good liar, especially whenever I got caught doing something I should not have been doing.

I could lie my way out of almost anything, I was so good at lying until sometimes I started to believe my own lies. I was a sneak thief and stabbing a friend in the back didn't bother me at all, especially if it meant getting out of some predicament I'd gotten myself into. What I'm trying to say is, I was not a very nice person. When you add alcohol to the mix, you have someone you don't want to be around. I was on my way to becoming the kind of person everyone said I was. I was able to get away with a lot of stuff, because Mom was easy; many times, she let me off the hook when I should have been punished. She would feel sorry for me and let me off until the next time. Unlike Grandma, she never followed through on her promise to get me later.

On the other hand, my new stepfather was not as gullible as my mother. So I would avoid him when I could, but when he called me out on something, I usually played dumb (like I didn't know what I was doing), or that what I was doing was what all the other kids were doing. He didn't buy into it like Mom.

My dad was very shrewd as well. He used to set traps that would alert him if anyone went into his room or touched any of his belongings: a piece of string lying on a bottle, or a pencil lying a certain way in his desk drawer. He went as far as to mark his liquor bottles when he realized that someone was rambling through his closet. He was clever, but I caught on to him. If he asked if someone had touched something in his desk drawer or in his closet, I would lie and tell him it must have been Aaron.

Aaron and my stepfather didn't get along well at all. For some reason, Aaron didn't like him and he let it be known. He was always doing just the opposite of what Dad would tell him to do.

Aaron was also a kid of determination. If he saw something he wanted, he would find a way to get it. He saved up enough money from his paper route sales to purchase a 1946 Ford when he turned sixteen. He was also a person who loved to fish. One night, he and two or three of his friends were out fishing, and they spotted a boat and motor tied up by the dock of a home that was a few miles from our home. That night, they went back and stole the boat, oars, and motor. They hid the boat in some bushes then took the boat and motor home. When they went fishing, they would haul the motor back and forth in my brother's wagon that he used to deliver his papers. I don't know how long they had the boat, but one night, as they were coming back from a fishing trip, a railroad detective stopped them and inquired about the motor and oars they had in the wagon. The detective had been alerted to be on the lookout for anyone acting suspicious because there had been several motors stolen off boats in the nearby area.

What happened next is why I always chose to be by myself if I was going to do something that might land me in jail. When the detective approached them and asked about the motor, one of the boys with them, JD, began spilling out everything he knew. He told the detective that he was not with them when they stole it, and that he had nothing to do with it. He even volunteered to show the detective where the boat was hidden (which, by the way, the detective knew nothing about the boat).

By the time JD had finished spilling everything he knew, my brother and his friend were arrested and I found out later, since I was not with them, that they went to jail and my stepdad had to go down and get them out at 2 a.m.. Needless to say, my stepdad was not happy

From that time on, things only got worse between Aaron and Dad. Aaron would stay out past curfew and because he knew Dad would not let him in, he would knock on my mother's window and she would get up and let him in the front door.

Because of the nature of my father's business, people came to the house at all hours of the night, so Mom slept in a separate room in the front of the house, so as not to be disturbed every time someone came to play a number.

One night, Aaron came home plastered and threw up behind the bed. He must have been seventeen or eighteen years old at the time. My dad was out on a late night call, so Mom came in and tried to clean up the mess and quiet Aaron down before Dad returned. Mom didn't want Dad to know because he would have taken a different approach to the situation.

This started happening more and more until one night, Aaron came home drunk, Dad confronted him, and Aaron cursed him out.

My Dad owned a .45 automatic, but he didn't always keep it in the house. When Aaron cursed him out, Dad was in his pajamas getting ready for bed. The next thing I knew, he was getting dressed and putting on his shoes. I knew what that meant. My dad suffered from emphysema and a weak heart so physical confrontation was out of the question for him. He got dressed, and left the house.

I told Aaron the best thing he could do was get out of there as fast as he could and my mother agreed. We got him up on his feet and I took him over to a neighbor's house, where he spent the night. I got back home just before Dad walked into the house and came directly to our room. He was huffing and puffing; and his Irish blood made it look like he was going to explode any minute. I had only seen him this angry on one other occasion and that was when some street hood tried to rob him.

Dad was a good man, but he didn't take guff off anybody. We finally got him calmed down, told him Aaron was gone and would not be coming back. Dad left the house again. When he came back, the bulge under his shirt was gone.

Just to explain the kind of man my dad was, one night, he was walking home, as always, he had a pocket full of money (due to the nature of his business).

A would-be robber approached him a couple of blocks from our house and demanded that Dad give up his money. Dad refused.

The gunman said, "If you don't give me your money, I'm going to shoot you." Dad still refused and told the gunman to do whatever he had to do because he was not going to give him his money. The gunman shot him in the thigh and Dad fell to the ground. The gunman said, "Now give me your money." Dad still refused. Dad said, "You may as well kill me, because that's the only way you're going to get anything off me."

Just as the gunman started to shoot again, someone yelled, the would-be robber panicked and took off running. Dad then got up, walked home, and called a doctor friend (who had lost his license for malpractice). Doc came over and took care of Dad.

Unfortunately for Aaron, he would never be able to control his drinking. A week before his fortieth birthday, he was killed in an automobile accident while under the influence of alcohol.

How It Began

As a youngster from the age of nine or ten and through most of my teenage years, I was not a happy person unless I was drinking. My fear of people and my lack of self-confidence made it almost impossible for me to excel at anything. Extra activities at school, such as sports, music or anything that required my being at school after the 3:00 p.m. bell rang, were of no interest to me. For the most part, I didn't have any real friends. Most of the guys with whom I spent time usually left me to myself once my money ran out or the booze was gone.

I spent a large amount of time fantasizing about being someone other than who I was. I used to envy the other boys, especially those who had girlfriends, and the ones who were popular at school.

Although some of the kids tolerated having me around, almost no one really liked me and I didn't like myself. I hated my life and who I was. If only I wasn't so shy and afraid. If only I had some skills or could dance or was good at sports like the other guys. If only, if only, if only. It was the story of my life.

The only way for me to escape the pain of loneliness and fear was to drink, and drink I did. Drinking was the only thing I felt I could do as well as anyone else.

Alcohol gave me the courage to do, and say, the things I would not normally say or do. I was a scared little boy (who learned early how to swear louder than most adults) to hide the fact that I was insecure and afraid to be myself.

I became very good at hiding my true feelings behind my skill to verbally attack others and outswear anyone who chose to engage me in a battle of obscenities. I thought that if I cursed loud enough and acted mean enough, I could bluff my way out of any situation.

There was a stupid game that we used to play when I went to junior high school called the dirty dozens. Two people would engage in a contest to see who could make the other fellow feel the worst by talking about his opponent's mother.

I rarely lost, but didn't know when to quit. As I went after my opponent using every unthinkable curse word I knew, I would feed on the laughter of the crowd. It felt *good* to hear the kids laughing at someone else instead of at *me*. The more the crowd cheered me on, the more obscene I became with my verbal attacks. I would get caught up in the frenzy of the crowd and would not stop even thought my opponent would tell me he was through. As a matter of fact, my opponents would often tell me that if I said one more thing about their mother, they would flatten me. This usually made me be quiet because physical confrontation was not something I wanted to engage in.

It wasn't long after discovering Dad's hideaway for his liquor, that I became a regular visitor to his closet every time I got the chance. For fear of being found out, I decided I needed another source from which to get my liquor. So I would go up to the corner (a place where people gathered, who had nothing better to do), and stand around by the liquor store where I could always find an adult who would gladly purchase a pint for me if I bought one for him.

Pontiac was a factory town and the favorite pastime of many of the people in my community was drinking. It wasn't hard to find someone willing to go into the store and get me a bottle.

After a while, I became friends with the store owner. She would sell it to me even though she knew I was under age. I was very good at getting people to do what I wanted them to do for me. I had become a master at manipulation and deceiving.

Before my brother lost his mind and cursed out our dad, he had a paper route. On many Friday nights after he went to bed, I would visit his pockets and relieve him of a few dollars of his paper-route collection money. When he discovered his loss the next morning, he would accuse me of taking his money. Of course, I would lie and deny it. By selling the cigarettes I stole from the vending machines and taking money I used to find in my mother's purse, (which she always left standing open), I could support my drinking habit well.

From age ten through the age of twelve, I used to drink only when I would be away from home, never around my parents. But as I grew into my teenage years and my need to suppress my fears became greater, I would drink as often as I could. The years clicked by and when I was fourteen or fifteen, my stealing and (lying to cover my tracks) had escalated to breaking into school lockers; and breaking-and-entering neighborhood businesses to steal money. I was nothing but a thief who would do whatever I needed to do to get money for my drinking.

In those days, the neighborhood I lived in was noted for being one of the toughest areas in the city, especially the street where I lived. This was mainly because there were so many kids of all ages in my neighborhood. I had the reputation of being a "tough guy" outside of my neighborhood to those who didn't know me. I could fool a lot of people for a long time by pretending to be tough when I was only a bully who took pride in taking advantage of the younger kids. Whenever I was confronted by someone my own age or size, I would most often back down—unless I was drinking. If I was drinking, it didn't matter how big or how many, I would take them all on.

When I was around the age of fifteen years old, I used to skip school a lot. One year during my first year in high school, I skipped the whole semester of afternoon classes. I'd go to a friend's house whose parents worked during the day and we would drink and watch TV.

Several other delinquents (like me) would gather at another one of my friend's home after his parents had gone work and we would shoot pool in his basement until it was time for school to let out. Skipping school was not uncommon for a lot of the kids I hung out with.

Mr. Buddy

One day, one of my friend's neighbors, whom I will call Mr. Buddy, was outside painting his home. As I was getting ready to leave and go home, Mr. Buddy called me over and asked if I would hold his ladder while he climbed up to paint around the gutters. He told me he would pay me; this was all I needed to hear. So I went over, and held the ladder for him. I don't know if he knew I had been drinking or not, but, if he did, he didn't let on that he knew.

When he finished for the day, he asked if I would come back the next day (which was a Saturday) and help him until he finished the job. I told him I would—and I did. This was the beginning of a friendship between us that would grow far beyond what I could have imagined.

Mr. Buddy was to have a tremendous impact on my life. He planted some seeds of confidence and self-esteem in me that would lie dormant for almost six years. Gradually, the things Mr. Buddy taught me helped lead a seriously troubled young man away from the road to self-destruction on which I was traveling.

Mr. Buddy was married to a beautiful lady named Bertha. The two of them lived about a block over from where we lived. They had a grown daughter who lived in Chicago with her husband. Mr. Buddy had suffered a childhood disease, which had left him unable to bend one of his legs. He walked with a limp, but, believe me, he was not handicapped.

He had recently purchased a vacant house not too far from us and was in the process of renovating it. One day after I had finished mowing his lawn, he asked if I would like to help him work on his new house. He was going to fix it up, then sell it to his sister.

I agreed to help him and started to spend a lot of time around Mr. Buddy. Years later, he would share with me that he never really needed my help; his goal was to draw me away from the boys with whom I was spending my free time. He told me he had seen something in me (that told him) I didn't belong with them.

I thank God for bringing Mr. Buddy into my life, because every one of the boys in that group of friends died before they became thirty years old. Most of them had died from drug overdoses. Two died after being shot while trying to rob a gas station.

Mr. Buddy was a mentor to me. When we were working together, he was always teaching me about being responsible and doing what <u>was</u> right, rather than always following the crowd. He taught me the importance of keeping my appearance up and of being well-groomed.

One thing I remember was how he used to instill in me the importance of completing any task I set out to do. He used to say, "If a task is once begun, never leave it till it's done. Be the labor great or small, do it well or not at all."

I believe he started telling me this, because, in the beginning of our relationship, my work ethic was not very good. I was only half doing some of the things he assigned me to do. I eventually began to spend most of my free time with Mr. Buddy even when we were not working. I would go over to his home and just spend time with him and his wife, whom I began to call Ma Bertha.

Mr. Buddy noticed I didn't get my hair cut on a regular basis, so he made a deal with his barber to cut my hair every two weeks; he even suggested the way he thought I should wear it. Mr. Buddy would pay for it when he went in to get his hair cut. All I had to do was walk into the shop, take a seat in the chair, get my hair cut, say thank you, and walk out.

He showed me where he kept emergency money in a little drawer in his kitchen. He told me that if I ever needed anything, or had an emergency where I needed some money (and had nowhere else to get it), I could take it from the drawer. Since they never locked their doors, I was invited to stop by anytime, even if they were not home. I never abused the privilege nor misused his trust; I never took anything from the drawer. Not that I wasn't tempted on more than one occasion.

Our relationship grew; we became very close. I appreciated being included in all of their family activities.

His beautiful daughter (*and I do mean beautiful*) was at least ten years older than I was; I loved to be there when she came home to visit. I had a *real* young boy's crush on her for a while. Years later, after her parents had passed on, I kept in touch with her by phone until she moved to Florida. I have not able to locate her, nor have I spoken to her since 2001.

In my own home, verbal, as well as physical expressions of love, were uncommon. There was no physical touching, nor words of affirmation; we didn't hug a lot. Rarely did I hear the words, "I love you." I guess this is the reason I found it hard to express my real feelings to another person for many years. Saying "I love you" just didn't sound right to me. For a while, things were going well. Even though I stopped hanging out with the boys next door to Mr. Buddy, I still had some drinking buddies on my block. I was living a double life: when I was around Mr. Buddy and my parents, I was one person, but once I got out of their sight, the bad side of me showed up.

Sometimes when my brother and I were in our room after bedtime, some of our friends, who could stay out later than we were allowed, would come to our bedroom window with a fifth or two of wine. We would hang out the window and drink.

One night when one of the guys was making too much noise, my stepfather almost shot him because Dad thought someone was trying to break into the house.

After that incident, we found another place to meet. Sometimes, we would sneak out of the window, go get plastered, and then sneak back into our room.

When I turned sixteen years old, I lost all interest in school. I kept going because I knew I would graduate the next year if I just "hung in and toughed it out." One day, I got into an argument over an assignment I didn't complete with one of my teachers. I got up out of my seat, walked out of class, and never went back. I continued to leave home every morning as if I was going to school, but most of the time, I would go hang out in the pool room or go over to a friend's house and drink alcohol.

After dropping out of school, I felt so bad and was so ashamed that I could not face Mr. Buddy. I stopped going by his house. When he showed up at my door, I would run out the back, then run up the street to hide until he left.

Whenever I was out walking, I would always keep my eye open to be on the look-out for him. He had the only old 47 Chevrolet in town, which could easily be spotted a long way off.

One day, about a year after I had dropped out of school, I was walking home from my neighbor Mark's garage, which was about three quarters of a mile from my house. I used to spend a lot of time at the garage doing odd jobs, and working on cars to make extra money.

Suddenly, I looked up and saw Mr. Buddy driving down the road toward me. I was trapped with no place to hide. There were no buildings, trees, or anything for me to duck behind.

As he came closer, he recognized me. I was just about to cross the street when I saw his car swerve to the left then turn right in front of me.

He stopped, got out, and came over to me. He hugged me and told me he was glad to see me. He invited me over to his home as though nothing had ever happened. He never mentioned anything about my dropping out of school or how I suddenly disappeared and had broken off contact with him giving no explanation.

Now I know how the prodigal son must have felt when his Father came out to meet him. At that time, I didn't know anything about the Bible; but later when I read Luke

15, I could identify with that young lad. Mr. Buddy treated me the same way the prodigal son's father had treated his son. After our meeting that day, I began to visit Mr. Buddy's home but not the same way I had before I screwed up.

I stopped by occasionally but I didn't spend as much time with them like I had before.

I owe a lot to Mr. Buddy and Ma Bertha. Unfortunately, he never lived to see how his investment in me paid off. He passed away before the Lord took hold of me and turned my life around.

The day I graduated from college with a degree in Bachelor of Arts in Business Administration, I sent a copy of my diploma to Ma Bertha. I continued to stay in touch with her until she passed away in 2001. I was in the final year of graduate school when she passed. Every time I would talk with her, I would tell her how grateful I was, for all they had done for me back in my teen years.

Moving Out

When I turned eighteen years old, I decided that I wanted to strike out on my own. I went to Dad and told him I was thinking about moving out. I wanted to leave on good terms with him, because if things didn't work out for me, I would be able to return. It was a good thing I did, because I did have to go back for a short time.

After making sure the door would be open for me if I should have to come back, I packed my bags and rented a house with a friend of mine. My friend had left his wife and was looking for someone with whom to share the cost of rent.

Both of us had ideas of our own about making money. At that time, my only job was helping to run a combination pool room and gambling joint.

Life on my own was good—at first. I was a pretty good gambler and pool hustler; the money I held back (when my boss was not around during a big game) gave me a nice income.

One day after my boss found out I was dating one of his girlfriends, he never let on that he knew, but he manufactured a reason to fire me. So, my friend and I decided to open our own joint and run it out of our house. The money began pouring in and things were going well. We partied around the clock; drinking all day was a way of life for me.

One night, my friend and I had been to a dance, returning home with two young ladies. I was in my room, and he was in his. It was around two or three in the morning when I heard this loud commotion going on out in the gambling area. I got up, opened my door, and looked directly into the face of my friend's wife, (whom he had supposedly left). As it turned out, he had secretly moved back into his home—but he had never told me.

Now, let me describe his wife to you. Put it like this: if I were to come upon his wife and a grizzly bear in a wrestling match, I would help the bear. She was one of the meanest and toughest woman I have ever known. No one, and I mean *no one*, ever messed with her, not even my friend. I saw her in a fight one day and it took four policemen to get her off the guy she was fighting, and he was a lot bigger and older than her.

She asked me where he was, then pushed me out of her way so she could look around my room. Satisfied that he was not there, she stomped out and marched off, going back to his room where she began to gather up everything he owned, and throwing it on the bed. In one fell swoop, she gathered the four corners of the sheets, and following through, she scooped up the whole bundle and headed for the door. On her way out, she turned to me and said, "Tell him his stuff is at home where I'll be waiting for him!" With that, she turned and was gone.

When all of this started, I was still a little high from the alcohol and barbiturates I had consumed earlier. The site of her, plus all the excitement, had cleared my head. I had to smoke a joint just to try and relax. I went inside his room and noticed the window was open. I figured he and the girl had made a quick exit at the moment his wife burst in the front door.

About five minutes after she left, I heard a knocking on my bedroom window. I looked out to see him along with the girl. I let them in, asking him what was going on. That's when he told me that he had moved back in with his wife. After that night, when word got out about what had happened, our business began to fall off because people were afraid to gamble at our place; they were afraid his wife might send the police in to raid us. Meanwhile, he moved back home full time and left me holding the bag for all the rent. It wasn't long before I got behind and couldn't make the rent payments. I moved out and moved in with my friend Mark who was renting a house on the other side of town. I stayed there for a short time, but he was about to get evicted, so I went to see my dad and moved back home.

Greetings, Uncle Sam Wants You!

After being on my own for almost two and a half years, it was hard to live under my parents' rules. But as it turned out, I didn't have to very long.

A couple of months after I returned home, I received a letter from the Selective Services Department directing me to report for my physical exam at Fort Wayne, 6325 Jefferson Ave., in Detroit. I was inducted into the army on October 8, 1964, and sent to Fort Knox, Kentucky.

When I left home to take my physical, I was under the impression that I would be returning home. No such luck. After the physical and we took the oath of commitment, we were loaded onto a bus and shipped off to basic training camp. Mentally, I was not prepared for this and my attitude created many unnecessary problems in the first few days after my induction.

For one, I was not used to taking orders; every time I was ordered to do something, I responded as if I was still a civilian, which was when I got ready. This attitude didn't go over too well with the officers who were giving the orders.

That first night in the barracks after the lights went out, I heard a lot of young boys crying. Some of these kids were only seventeen and eighteen years old, probably the first time they had been away from home.

After being yelled at and disciplined a few times, I finally made up my mind to shape up, follow orders, and get the next two years over with as easy as I could make it.

In the fifth week of basic training during an afternoon session of physical training, I collapsed on the training field. I spent the next two weeks in the army hospital where I was diagnosed with double pneumonia. I was introduced to army cold medicine, otherwise known as "GI Gin."

I became addicted to the stuff. I caught pneumonia at least five more times (on purpose) just so I could go to the hospital and get my "medicine." It was truly amazing! Some of the stupid things I did when I was young. Today, I have a chronic cough that has plagued me for over fifty years and I think it is largely because of the way I treated my body when I was younger.

Pneumonia patients were the work force in sick bay. Once the fever dropped, you were assigned a job as a maintenance worker. Each morning you got up, made your bed, and collected your dust mop, or mop bucket and mop, and went off to clean some part of the hospital.

When the authorities realized I was shamming to get out of duty, they discharged me from the hospital and sent me back to my unit to finish boot camp.

Meanwhile, all of my original friends whom I had met when I first was inducted had already shipped out to other assignments.

After boot camp, I was sent to Fort Sill, Oklahoma, for four weeks of Advanced Individual Training (AIT). After that, I was transferred to Fort Dix, New Jersey, and was soon put on a ship headed overseas to Erlangen, Germany.

While in Fort Sill, I received a letter from my girl-friend (the mother of my son), telling me she was expecting another baby, that she was dating someone else, and it was over between us. I took this hard because I loved her and had planned on getting married when I got back home.

I was drinking and up past curfew when the charge of quarters (CQ) came in and ordered me to bed. I cursed him out and took a swing at him when he tried to push me toward my bunk. Not a good thing to do. I received my first and only Article 15.

The trip to Germany was, by far, a whole lot worse than the bus ride from Tennessee to Michigan. There were about two thousand troops on board that ship, some with their families. Many of us spent the trip hanging over the rail. I have never been so sick in my life. I lost almost twenty pounds in the seven days it took to get to Germany.

THOMAS E. TARPLEY SR.

The only things I could eat were peanuts and saltine crackers. They only stayed down for a few minutes before I had to lean over the rail, soon making my deposit into the black waters of the Atlantic.

About three or four days out, we ran into a storm. The waves were higher than the ship; I was more miserable than from any hangover I had ever experienced.

All I wanted was to get my feet on some dry land; at that point, they could have left me on an island—I would not have objected. I made up my mind then and there, if I didn't die first, I would never get on another boat as long as I lived!

If the authorities had any intentions of sending me back home by ship, they could forget it. I would take a European discharge and pay my own way home on a plane.

Near the end of the trip overseas, the water calmed and the ship seemed to not be moving; although it took a while, my stomach began to feel better and I was able to eat some real food after a day or so.

Welcome to Bremerhaven

T he ship docked in Bremerhaven, Germany, and the water was finally calm enough for my stomach to completely settle down. I don't recall how long a time we spent there; I also can't remember if we transferred to a truck or a train; or if we continued the journey by ship.

When we finally arrived in Erlangen, Germany, we were assigned to our barracks and given our duty assignments; I was assigned to *A*-Battery of the First Battalion and Thirty-Sixth Field Artillery.

After unpacking and getting my area in order, some of the other guys and I went out to explore the town. Naturally, our first stop was the Enlisted Men's (EM) Club.

Get this! A shot of liquor was only twenty-five cents; beer was fifteen cents a bottle. I thought this was the best thing that could have happened to me! If you had a class six card, you could buy a quart of liquor for $1.65 from the PX. What a place for an alcoholic (like me) to be!

Now, I may have been a drunk, but I was very clever; and always had some kind of scheme up my sleeve. I was a schemer, a manipulator, a liar, a thief and a con artist; and a few other things I dare not mention in this book. I had all the qualifications of a person you least likely wanted your daughter to meet.

As soon as I arrived at my unit in Germany, I found a way to get sent on special duty assignment for twelve of the fourteen months I was supposed to be over there. I knew I didn't want to have anything to do with the motor pool or the heavy artillery. My unit was an eight-inch how-itzer unit; the gun weighed fifty-four tons. The projectile weighed over two hundred pounds while the powder used to fire the mammoth weapon was about thirty-five pounds. This assignment was not for me.

I managed to get a special duty assignment, which required me to work with the Military Police Detachment. Our job was to provide post security. All we had to do was guard the three access gates to the post. Occasionally, we would go downtown and bring back a few GIs who had consumed too much beer.

There was one other assignment that I was lucky enough to get even after I had stopped a colonel and made him show me his ID.

The colonel was in civilian clothes when he tried to enter the post through my gate. He was on a bicycle and tried to ride right by me without stopping. So I yelled at him to halt. He stopped and came back and I asked for his identification. He got indignant and became very angry. He seemed to have been drinking and he proceeded to curse at me, but he never identified himself.

The gate I was working was right across from the post theater and there was an army captain in uniform standing in line waiting for the movie to open. He noticed what was going on and ran over to the gate and told me that the man was Colonel Black, the post commander. I told him I didn't care who he was, my orders were to stop anyone not in uniform and check their identification.

This was not the best way I could have handled the situation but something about having a loaded .45 automatic on my side gave me a sense of power. A few minutes later, my commanding officer showed up and relieved me of duty and told me to go back to the barracks and wait for him. When he arrived, he informed me that I would no longer be working the gates, and that I would be sent back to my unit. I asked why and he told me Colonel Black told him to send me back.

The army newspaper, *The Stars and Stripes*, was always looking for a good story, so I told my commanding officer that I was going to call them and tell them how I was relieved from duty because I followed the orders given to me by my superior.

The next day, I was told that I would not be going back to my unit, and I was going to have a new assignment.

This new assignment was from eight in the morning to four in the afternoon. All I had to do was sit in the commissary and check ID cards of anyone who came in that was not in uniform. I liked this job because most of the customers were wives of military personnel whose husbands were out in the field or *somewhere* working on a piece of machinery. I had it made; and because of my job, I met a lot of people who knew how to make money. They were willing to invest in me and help me get my own business started. I became a loan shark.

The going interest rate on post was eighty percent. The closer to payday, the higher the interest rate; for instance, a week before payday, interest was 100 percent. A twenty-dollar loan was to be paid back in the amount of forty dollars—thereby doubling my money. It was a good business; a lot of people made big bucks, including me.

My tour in Germany was fun for me. It went by very quickly. Because of my special duty assignment, I didn't have to go into the field or play soldier boy. Although, I was officially attached to the artillery division, I never saw any duty in my company until a couple of months before I was to return home. I spent my days sitting in the commissary, flirting with women, and getting their phone numbers; my evenings were whiled away in the Enlisted Men's Club, drinking.

Everyone knew where to find me: it was important to be available—in case someone needed a loan. Occasionally, a couple of us would go out to the nearby towns and visit a guest house if we wanted to meet some of the German women.

Like all good things, mine suddenly came to an end when my battalion received orders to pull up stakes and move north to a new location about 150 miles away. I thought I had escaped moving with them because I had kept a low profile while they were in the process of getting ready to move. I watched from my window in the military police station as the trucks and big guns rolled out the front gate. Two days after they left, my commanding officer called the MP headquarters and told the sergeant they had forgotten the colonel's staff sedan in the motor pool. He told the sergeant to put me in it, with all my belongings, and point me north. Thus, went my smooth ride; in a way, it was a good thing because a lot of the guys who owed me money had moved north to the new location. Some of them were not very happy to see me when I got to the new post.

When I arrived at my new post in Neu-Ulm, I was assigned the job of being a gun driver. I had never even been in the cockpit, let alone having driven one; that didn't seem to matter to my sergeant. He simply told one of the other drivers to show me my gun and teach me what I needed to know.

The next thirty days were torture. We moved out into the training fields and had to sleep in foxholes and tents. It was cold, which of course I was not used to, nor did I know anything about what was going on.

I finally conned my way into changing jobs with an army personnel carrier (APC) driver. This move helped me escape from all the noise of big guns going off, and I was no longer handling the two hundred-pound projectiles, which had to be loaded by hand. My new job consisted of me sitting in my APC on perimeter guard duty; I had my liquor and all I could eat.

Each APC was stocked with a supply of emergency food called *C*-rations. These cases were tightly wired, which took a wire cutter to open them. But I found a way around that. I used my field can opener, and, where the wire was connected, I carefully unraveled it and slid it off the box. I would then open the box, eat what I wanted, and then replace the wire; putting the box back in place with no one realizing the difference. I even passed inspection one day when a colonel showed up unexpectedly by helicopter wanting to inspect the troops and the field artillery. Over the next few weeks, I managed to empty nine cases of

C-rations. As far as I know, when I left the unit to return home, no one ever knew the difference.

Being out in the field was also good for my loan business. Some guys would borrow money to go into the nearby towns; they didn't mind paying one hundred percent interest. I would usually hold back my money until all the other sharks were out of money; then I would name my own terms.

I loaned out as much as two to three thousand dollars a week before payday and collected double a week later. I didn't have a problem collecting like some of the other guys did, because I hired a couple of bruisers as collection agents. On payday, I was the first person my customers saw when they walked out of the payroll office. Reluctantly, they would pay me off. I would then loan it back to them at the eighty percent interest rate. Many of my regular customers were only able to pay the interest; very few ever paid off the principle.

One day while having lunch, I was sitting next to a friend who worked in Headquarters Battery. He had driven out to the location where we were to conduct some official army business. I was telling him how anxious I was to get out of Germany and asked if he could help me. He said he could—for a price. I slipped him two hundred dollars and two days after he got back to battalion headquarters, I received orders that I was to be in Munich a week later to await deployment back to the States. I found a couple of other sharks stationed on base and sold them my collection notebook. I then notified all my (now former) clients that I was leaving and that I had transferred their debts to the new owners.

After clearing up a few loose ends and selling everything I couldn't take with me, I boarded a train for Munich. My friend got me off the base, but my flight date to the States didn't change, so I spent a couple of weeks partying in Munich.

Back In the States

I arrived back in the States at Fort Dix, New Jersey, on September 14, 1966, and was officially separated from the army one day after arrival.

The first changes I noticed were the prices of cigarettes and of liquor. The amount I had been used to paying for a quart of liquor in Germany, I now paid for a shot. Cigarettes, which were fifteen cents in Germany, cost sixty to seventy-five cents stateside.

I got home to Pontiac about two weeks later after spending some time in New York. It was on a Friday night; and after hanging around the house with my family for a couple of hours, I took off to look up my old friends. It was as though two years had not passed. Everything was exactly like it was before I left; the same old people doing the same old thing.

On Monday, my brother, Aaron, asked if I would like to ride with him out to General Motors (GMC) to put in an application for a job. I had nothing better to do, so I went with him. Since I was there, I decided to put in an application myself, because I planned to go to work in about a month. Guess what? They turned him down but told me to come back that night at 3:00 p.m. for the second shift.

So, two days after getting home, I found myself with a job, which I didn't want because I had not had enough time to enjoy being home. I worked the afternoon shift for ninety days and on the day after I got my ninety days in, I went on sick leave; and with the help of a crooked doctor, who eventually lost his license for malpractice, for the next two and a half years, I stayed on sick leave.

One thing I need to include in this story is after returning from the military, I picked up a couple of new habits. I started smoking marijuana and popping pills like candy. Add that to the drinking and you have a walking zombie. This lifestyle was to go on for the next twenty-three years. I can't say it was fortunate or unfortunate, but I never lost a job because of my drinking. I am what people call a functioning alcoholic.

Shortly after I got home, my next door neighbor introduced me to one of her girlfriends. She thought I was a nice guy; I thought she was an honest lady. It turned out that we were both wrong. We dated for almost two years deciding in 1968 to get married. We decided to do so even though we argued and fought on a regular basis, mostly because of my drinking.

In 1970, we were blessed with a baby girl. This was my second child; I already had a son from a previous relationship who was four years old. He was born three months before I went into the military.

After being home from overseas for about a year, I could have been classified as a full-blown junkie. My consumption of alcohol, barbiturates, and marijuana was unbelievable. I don't know how I managed to escape killing myself or someone else. Every time I got behind the wheel of my car, I was legally drunk.

As I reflect on those days, the only conclusion I can make is that God had a plan laid out for my life and he was not going to let me screw it up. There were times when I knew I should have died from a drug overdose or because someone had put a bullet in me for something I had done to them.

Three years after hiring in to GMC, staying on sick leave for most of those years, I walked into my foreman's office and quit. I had had enough of the running back and forth to the doctor; besides, I hated being inside the plant for eight hours a day.

Shortly after I quit, my brother Aaron, who was working for a property management company as a site maintenance person, got his company to hire me part-time to help him do some painting at his complex. I continued to work for him after the job was completed. A year later, I was offered the opportunity to take over as manager of my own complex. This would necessitate moving out of Pontiac to Detroit; I accepted the offer, and in October of 1970, one month after our daughter was born, my wife and new baby girl pulled up stakes and moved to Detroit.

I liked living in Detroit, and, from the time I arrived, my supervisor, who loved to party, and I got along great together. I did my job, and he kept me supplied with weed and alcohol.

I had a key to his apartment. (Matter of fact, I had a key to everyone's apartment) and sometimes I would go over to his place after he went to work and raid his stash of marijuana and liquor. After working hours, we spent a lot of time together partying.

In 1972, my wife couldn't take anymore so she took my daughter and moved back to Pontiac. I would go out and see them occasionally, but I knew our marriage was beyond repair. It didn't bother me because I was seeing several other women at the time. Being an apartment manager had its advantages; there were a lot of single women in my complex.

About a month or two before my wife left me for the last time, I started to notice a young single woman whom I had known of since she had moved in to my complex; but I had never taken an interest in her. One day, she turned in a work order to have some repairs done to her unit. I must have awakened her when I rang her doorbell the morning I went to take care of the repairs in her unit. As I was working in her apartment, I noticed her lying across her bed. Although she had a robe on, I could see her legs and they were nice. Her name was Gloria; she worked for Western Union.

A New Way of Living

One day, I needed to send some money to a friend in California, so I went by Gloria's apartment to ask her if she could help me. I asked her if she would like to go out; later that night, we went out for the first time. After that, we started to spend time together; that was the beginning of a slow end to my life of hell-raising and rabble-rousing.

She was like no one I had ever dated and, for a long time, I thought she was perfect. She was quiet, patient, and she seemed to care about me. Whenever I would have my kids for the weekend, she would treat them like her own. Later, after I had gotten custody of them, they came to live with me on a permanent basis and she devoted a lot of time to helping me raise them. But even having the new responsibility of raising my children did not completely slow me down from my life on the wild side.

As I began to spend more time with Gloria, I broke off my relationships with the other women I was seeing. Gloria and I dated for almost three years before I asked her to marry me. At that time, my divorce from my previous wife had been final for only about six months. At the last minute, I began to have second thoughts, and tried to weasel out of my proposal, but she wouldn't let me.

So, on September 27, 1975, we were joined in holy matrimony. Despite my drinking, I have always treated my wife with respect. I was, and still am, very much in love with her. I kept trying to change her, to get her to act like me; it took several years for me to realize that she was not the one who needed to change!

Shortly after we were married, I developed another habit: snorting cocaine. I was running with the big boys; cocaine was their drug of choice. So I started using cocaine as well as still drinking heavily. I also continued to use all the other drugs I had been abusing for years.

One night, I was visiting a friend who used to call me his "brother." We were snorting cocaine and drinking when I noticed a strange taste in my mouth. It didn't take long for me to realize it was heroin. My so-called brother was trying to hook me on heroin by adding it to the cocaine. When I realized what was happening, it infuriated me. I came close to sending him into the next world—because he knew how I felt about heroin and he knew it was the one drug I never used.

Fortunately for me, I had tried it a few years earlier, so I would know what it tasted like if anyone ever tried to pass it off on me as cocaine. After sitting there steaming, trying to decide if I should pull out the .44 Magnum I had in my belt and put him out of his misery, I decided he wasn't worth my going to jail; so I left. I have never spoken to him again.

When I got home that night, I told Gloria what had happened. I started to think that maybe it was time for me to quit using the hard drugs, because if you could not trust your friends—then whom could you trust? Although I tried to slow down, I didn't stop. I continued to get high and drink. On top of that, I started lying to Gloria about the amount I was consuming. I would hide my liquor bottles and my drugs in our house. When I used at home, I wouldn't let her see me.

We had been married about five years when a great opportunity came along. As I have stated, I was a functioning alcoholic. I always did my job very well, thanks to Mr. Buddy. The top management company in the area heard about me and offered me a job in property management. Although it would mean a sizable pay cut in the beginning, I took the job because I saw opportunities that would make up for the temporary loss of income.

With the changing of jobs, it also meant we had to move because my old job came with a rent-free apartment. I gave my notice and started looking for a new home. We found a beautiful house not too far from my new job. We contacted the realtor to see if we could make an offer.

I wanted that house but we were told that there was already an offer on the table. I prayed and made a deal with God. I told him that if he would get this house for us, I would give up hard drugs. The next day, the real estate agent called and said that the other deal had fallen through and if we still wanted the house, we could make another offer.

We did, and we got the house. After that, I was scared to get high because I didn't (and still don't) believe in lying to, or playing with God.

No More Drugs

G iving up the hard drugs was not as difficult as I thought it would be. I flushed all my weed and cocaine and have never used any illegal drugs since. However, my drinking intake went through the roof. Keep in mind, I promised God to give up the hard drugs; since drinking was legal, I rationalized that it was okay to continue drinking. Besides, I needed it to keep my fear under control.

No one can treat his or her body the way I treated mine and not suffer some consequences. I had been with my new company for almost four years, and things were not going well between my boss and me. About two years into my new job, I realized I had made a big mistake. Number one, my boss was an expert at intimidation. The use of this tactic was how he controlled his employees. He realized early on that this method would not work on me; for the most part, he left me alone because he had a specific need for me.

I was under a lot of pressure; I had bought both a new home and a new car soon after I had started working for him. I also had taken a big reduction in income. Secondly, he wouldn't give me a large enough raise so I could meet my financial obligations and I was not hustling or selling drugs anymore. We were getting behind in our bills.

I had the worst properties in the company; he would not allow me to hire the help I needed to get the job done. I started to get angry and wanted to quit; but I was afraid of losing everything we owned. The pressure got so bad that whenever I thought about him, or got near the office, my chest would hurt. He was the most arrogant and egotistical maniac I had ever met. I can't call him a bigot or a racist because he hated everybody. He would use you for as long as he had need for your services and once he didn't need you, he would manufacture some excuse to fire you.

I watched this happen, repeatedly, wondering when it would be my turn. I believe the only reason he hired me was because I was black and had a lot of connections with the Department of Housing and Urban Development (HUD). He needed someone to help him acquire some HUD-controlled properties. Once that was done, he had no need for me.

One morning, as I was sitting in the office of one of my complexes talking with the office manager, she noticed that I was rubbing my left arm and opening and closing my hand. She asked what was wrong; I told her it was nothing, that I had been having some numbness and pain in my left side. She insisted I go to the hospital to get checked out, but I shrugged off her suggestion even though I was experiencing pain and numbness in my chest and arm more and more frequently.

After I finished talking with her, I headed toward another complex. Just as I was passing Mount Carmel Hospital, a sharp pain hit me in the chest. I decided to go in and get checked out; I was there for ten days. Tests revealed I had had a silent heart attack sometime in the past and that there was damage to the back side of my heart. The doctor asked me if I drank—lying, I told him, "I occasionally took a sip." After running test after test and coming up with no conclusive answer, they told me my problem was probably stress related.

While I was in the hospital, my boss called wanting to know where the company car was. I told him it was at my house, parked out front. He asked where the keys were; I told him my wife had them. He said to call her and tell her someone would be by to pick it up; my position had been terminated.

Ordinarily, this would have been a bad thing; but the moment I hung up the phone, I started to feel better. It was as though a great weight had been lifted off my chest.

A couple of days after being released from the hospital, I went by my church to go over the bills. At that time, I was the treasurer. There was a letter addressed to me from a nationally known insurance company. They were looking for agents. Just for kicks, I filled out the reply card and mailed it back. I told Gloria about it; I said I only did it for the "heck of it." I said to her, "I am not a salesman." To which she replied, "Oh yes, you are!"

A couple of days later, the district manager from the insurance office in my area, called and asked me to come in for an interview; so, I went. The interview went well. I was hired pending my obtaining all my insurance licenses. I proceeded to apply for, and receive, my licenses, and became a registered representative with the company. I was hired on my birthday in 1985; and I spent ten years with them. When I quit, I was doing very well. At one point, I was promoted to sales manager, but I found that working as an agent was more suited for me. I gave up the management position and went back out in the field.

My Walk to Emmaus

In 1989, something happened that made me stop and take a long look at my life. On July 29, 1989, I spent most of the night drinking with a couple of friends. The next morning, I woke up at home with no memory of what had happened the night before. This was not unusual as I was accustomed to having blackouts; but usually, the activities of the night before would come back to me.

Whatever happened that night is still a mystery. To this day, I do not know what occurred that night; other than the fact that I, along with two other friends, drank at least three and one half fifths of liquor. I have not had a drink of alcohol since that night.

While I was drying out, a good friend and (church member) kept pestering me to attend an Alcoholics Anonymous (AA) meeting with him. I finally consented (just to get him off my back), and went to my first AA meeting.

A funny thing happened at that meeting: I discovered something almost everyone else already *knew*, *I am an alco-*

holic. I have been an active member of the program of AA since that night, and on July 29, 2016, I celebrated twenty-seven years of sobriety.

In October of 1989, even though I was sober, I was experiencing some troubles in my life. I was losing interest in my church, and my marriage was about to break up. It was around that time when the associate pastor of my church suggested I go on a Walk to Emmaus. I had no idea what he was talking about.

I told him I didn't think it was for me. He continued to talk to me, explaining what went on at the weekend. After he told me if I didn't like it, I could call him and he would come and pick me up, I agreed to go. I thank God every day for moving me to go to that retreat. My life has not been the same since that weekend.

For the first time in my life, I felt the presence of the Holy Spirit; it was during that weekend that I made a commitment to God. I promised him that I would go wherever, be whatever, and do whatever he asked of me. I have never reneged on that promise; although I did come very close, especially after I received the call to move to Fowlerville, Michigan, from my United Methodist District superintendent.

During that Emmaus weekend, God sent another guardian angel into my life to help guide me along the right path. His name was Jerry. He and I both had a problem sleeping that first night. I was sitting on the steps in the hallway about three or four in the morning, trying to figure a way to get out of there, when Jerry came walking down the hallway toward me. I don't remember the conversation, but we have been very good friends since that night.

The next year, I received a call from the director of the Upper Room in Nashville, Tennessee, wanting to know if I would be interested in going on a trip to South Africa.

I thought surely the gods must be crazy. Knowing my fear of flying and my past history, I wondered whatever had possessed him to call me. A few years later, I found out that Jerry had put my name in the hat for a possible team member to be part of a group going to South Africa. This was scheduled to be a pilot program for the Walk to Emmaus. Jerry has continued to do things like that over the years. My life has been truly blessed by our friendship.

When I got home from my first Emmaus Walk, every time I thought about the unconditional love I received on that weekend retreat, I would burst into tears.

It was about two years later, in 1992, that I enrolled in Detroit Ecumenical Seminary in a two-year course in Christian Ministry to try to determine if God was calling me into full-time ministry.

I found my answer.

In 1995, shortly after I finished the diploma in Christian Ministry program, another insurance company began talking to me about the possibility of my coming to work for them.

I resigned from my old company and went to work for the new company. This new company promised me a lot of perks and bonuses, but after about a year with them, I saw that things were not materializing as they had been described to me. I began to look at other options._

In the process of looking for other options, I met an old acquaintance who was working for New York Life Insurance Company (NYLIC). After some discussion about perks and benefits, I applied for a job with them.

Changing to NYLIC was a wise choice: I had my own office suite and the commission scale was much better. Things were going well; I thought, *At last I have found my destiny.*

But God had other ideas. Even though I was making more money than ever, I started to lose interest in what I was doing. The job didn't excite me as it did in the beginning of my insurance career. Something was missing; deep down in my heart, I knew what it was. God was calling me into the ministry—and that was the very last thing I wanted to do.

While I was working on the largest case of my financial planning career, the words of Joshua kept coming to mind. "Choose ye this day whom you will serve." I couldn't get it out of my head. Then Jesus himself spoke to me in Matthew 6:24, "You cannot serve two masters."

That was it! I was trying to stay in the middle of the road, and God was saying, "It's time to choose up sides."

My dilemma was, I wanted to do what God wanted me to do, but I didn't want to give up the money (especially with me being so close to closing a case worth more than I had ever thought possible). One night, I could not bear the stress of indecision any longer, so I gave up and told the Lord, "Your will be done, not mine."

Almost instantly, I felt a peace come over me that I can't explain. In the next few weeks, I began making arrangements to go back to school and get my Bachelor's degree in Business Administration. I enrolled in an accelerated degree program in which you attend one night a week and every other Saturday.

Although I had enrolled in Cleary College and was preparing to enter seminary, I was still uncertain about the role ministry was to play in my life. There was no doubt in my mind that I was not ready to be a pastor. I had already decided that I would serve God from the ranks, but not out front. I volunteered for almost anything asked of me, as long as it didn't require a lot of public speaking. But, the more I dodged speaking assignments, the more people came to me and tried to get me to speak. It was becoming obvious to me that people were seeing something in me that I didn't see in myself.

While working on a Walk to Emmaus weekend in the spring of 1997, during my turn to speak, I shared my desire to attend Asbury Theological Seminary, but had chosen not to go because of the distance from my home and the cost of tuition. Although I had not yet resigned from my job with NYLIC, I knew that if I chose to go to seminary, I would have to give up my insurance job. I came up with the idea to keep working while attending Local Pastor's School instead. This way, I could keep my job, my home, and not have to give up anything.

One of the things I found out is that God's way of thinking (and mine) don't always run parallel to each other; sometimes I get ahead of God and take off on my own, then he must reel me back in.

After one of the training sessions, one of the team members whom I didn't know at the time, approached me and asked if he could talk with me. We went into one of the unoccupied rooms and he told me that he had talked with his pastor about what I had shared about wanting to go to Asbury, but had opted out in lieu of a different plan. He told me that his pastor told him I needed to go to Asbury; he then did something that brought me to tears. He took out a check, handed it to me, and said, "I know this won't cover all of your expenses, but my wife and I talked about it and we want to help you go to Asbury. We will be with you all the way. We will pay for all your books for as long as you are there."

At that time, I didn't wear my glasses all the time, only when I wanted to read. I could not see for how much the check was written, but I could make out a lot of zeroes. I put on my glasses and saw that the check was for a thousand dollars. Tears welled up in my eyes; I thanked him for his generosity. I told him if I didn't go, I would return the check.

It wasn't long after that that I surrendered to the call of God I felt on my life. I resigned from my position with NYLIC where I had been on track for having the best year of my insurance career. I accepted a position to become the part-time associate pastor of a church in the Detroit Cass Corridor even though my inner fears were running rampant, almost paralyzing me.

After the way I had lived my life, I felt so unworthy to be considering a position in which I would be telling people about God; in addition to trying to explain good and evil. I had absolutely no confidence in my ability to preach or teach; I didn't know the Bible well enough. I hated getting up in front of people to make a speech; plus I hated to go inside of hospitals to visit the sick.

The thing that most worried me (even more than my fear of failing), was how was I going to meet my financial obligations? My salary potential dropped from being a potential six-figure income to a low five-figure; to be exact, it was $10,840 per year.

In the next few months, I would pray my favorite Scripture verse, thousands of times as I lay awake at night trying to figure out where God was leading me. "Trust in the Lord God with all your heart and lean not unto your own understanding. In all your ways acknowledge Him and he will direct your path." (Prov. 3:5–6, NLT).

It was by faith, and faith alone, that I put my life in God's hands. I was committed to living up to the commitment I had made to him on my first Emmaus Walk, which was to be whatever he wanted me to be, to do whatever he called me to do and to go wherever he sent me.

What sealed my fate was what happened while working on another team for an Emmaus weekend. My friend Jerry, whom I met on my first walk, came walking up to me one Sunday afternoon with three other pastors. He said, "Let's go in the parlor where we can talk." I didn't like the sound of that, nor the look on the faces of the other three men; but I went with them into the parlor. Once inside, Jerry took his robe off and draped it over my shoulders; then he handed me one of his business cards, which had 1 Kings 19:19 hand-printed on the back. I asked him what this was all about. In answer, he said, "Read the Scripture." I picked up my Bible and looked up the passage. It read:

"So Elijah went and found Elisha the son of Shaphat plowing in a field. There were twelve teams of oxen in the field and Elisha was plowing with the twelfth team. Elijah went over to him and threw his cloak across his shoulders then walked away" (NLT).

Suddenly, that robe became very heavy and my knees began to get weak. I believe I dropped to my knees as all four of the pastors began to pray over me. As I realized what Jerry had just done, I was not sure I was ready for the responsibility.

Jerry was leaving the ministry; he had just transferred his responsibilities to me. All I could think of was, *God, when I made that commitment to you, this is not what I had in mind.*

When they were done praying, we all hugged—as I cried. Later that evening, when I got home, I showed the robe to Gloria and told her I thought I might be going into ordained ministry. She replied, "I already knew it."

She had always known when I'm about to do something, long before I do it.

Back to Kentucky

On February 5, 1998, I loaded up my car with as much as I could get into it (and still have a place to sit), kissed Gloria good-bye, and headed out to Wilmore, Kentucky.

It was a mild day for February, sunny and nearly forty degrees. As I traveled south on *I-75*, I noticed the weather was getting worse. By the time I had reached Ohio, the temperature had dropped considerably. When I crossed into Kentucky, I ran into the "blizzard of the century." Leave it to me to pick the one day Kentucky would get the largest snowfall on record for me to make my journey.

There was an accumulation of over twenty-two inches in a twenty-four-hour period. Driving was touch and go as I traveled the two-lane highway with bumper-to-bumper traffic for the last one hundred miles.

The trip took much longer than I had planned. By the time I arrived at the seminary, the admissions office was closed; the place was locked down tight.

I located a security person who gave me the keys to my apartment, which happened to be on the 3rd floor. Of course there was no elevator in the building.

As I was carrying my belongings up the stairs, a young female (who, as I later discovered, lived with her husband in the apartment next to mine) offered to help me; I gladly accepted her help. It didn't take us long, but climbing all those steps several times immediately following my extra-long snowy drive, finally drained me of all my energy. After thanking my neighbor, I went into my apartment and collapsed on the sofa.

Later that evening, after a few minutes of rest and after putting my belongings away, I sat down on the side of the bed, and thought, *What have you gotten yourself into now? What am I doing down here, next to nowhere, alone and more than a little bit afraid?*

I picked up the phone and called Gloria; it was really good to hear her voice. I wished she had come with me, but she was not quite ready to quit her job, move out of our home, and take up residence in another state without having some sort of idea as to what she was going to do. As for me, I had put all my trust in the promise God made to me in Proverbs 3:5–6, "Trust in the Lord with all your heart and lean not unto your own understanding. In all your ways acknowledge him and he will direct your path."

On the other hand, Gloria was not as willing to step out in faith as I was. She had a good-paying job, and she was not ready to give it up. It would take almost two months before she would decide that she could not live without me and decide to join me on campus.

Another thing that prompted her to join me was that she saw how "stressed" I was when I got home.

She knew that I was driving like a maniac, trying to get home in record time. By traveling with me, she thought she would be able to persuade me to take it easy, as taking driving breaks was better for both my heart and my circulation. She was right.

One thing that made my transition from Michigan to Kentucky a somewhat enjoyable experience is that a friend of mine (from the Emmaus community) was also attending seminary. After I finished talking with Gloria, I called him to let him know I had arrived in town. He came right over, took me to the local student hangout, and introduced me to some of the other students. The first thing I noticed was that most of them were young enough to be my grandchildren (I was fifty-five when I started seminary), but they made me feel right at home. In the next few days, my friend took me around town and showed me every place of local interest (which didn't take long).

The population in Wilmore was a little over 4500 with (2,900) two thirds of the population being made up of students. My friend drove me over to, and introduced me, as well, to a friend of Bill W., the founder of Alcoholics Anonymous. The next Tuesday, my new friend picked me up, and took me to my first Alcoholics Anonymous (AA) meeting in Wilmore.

Things were going as well as could be expected. I had selected and was attending my classes, but my trips back and forth to Michigan on the weekends kept me from participating in any of the weekend activities on campus. I didn't have another real option.

When I decided to go to seminary, I was working as a part-time associate pastor in the Cass Corridor. I had begun working there just after I had resigned my job with the New York Life Insurance Company. The salary was nowhere near what I had been making with NYLIC, but the church was also paying for my health insurance, which was over fifteen thousand dollars a year.

To keep my insurance, I made the decision to continue working at the church, which meant I had to drive home every weekend from Kentucky to preach the Sunday evening worship service. I owe a great deal of thanks to my supervising pastor who allowed me to stay employed while going to seminary.

My weekly routine was to leave Wilmore on Friday evening and arrive in Michigan early Saturday morning. This schedule gave me a chance to do some visiting and put the finishing touches on my sermon. After preaching on Sunday evening, I would get on the road around 9:00 or 9:30 p.m., then head back to Wilmore. I made the trip weekly for over three years and sometimes twice a week.

About two months after moving to Kentucky, Gloria and I realized that being separated all week was not good for us. She told me she was going to start bringing her resume up-to-date so she could begin to look for a job in Wilmore. This was good news to my ears because I missed her.

Now I will tell you about divine intervention. I began to tell people Gloria had decided to move down with me and that we were looking for a job for her. A couple of weeks later, after a long weekend in Michigan (I didn't have to be back to school until Tuesday morning), I arrived back on campus on Monday afternoon. After taking my things upstairs to my apartment, I went over to the Student Center Building where I knew everyone would be hanging out.

The moment I walked in the door, my neighbor (who lived on the second floor of my building) grabbed me by the arm and asked if Gloria had found a job yet. I told her, "No, we had just started looking."

She told me the director of admissions was looking for an administrative secretary at the Admissions Office. She almost dragged me across the courtyard to the admissions office where she inquired if they were still taking applications for the open position. The secretary told her that they had stopped accepting applications, but she would check with the director, to see if he would take one more. She came back and told us that if we could get it in before they closed that evening, he would take one more.

I took the application home and filled out most of it and then called Gloria to get the rest of the information I couldn't answer. I hurriedly ran back (yes, I could run then) to the Admissions Office and turned it in.

Now get this! Gloria called me that night and told me that the director of admissions called her that evening and asked if she could come in for an interview on Friday. I told her to call him back and tell him she could. Thursday morning I was in Detroit to pick her up. We drove back to Kentucky that evening, and Friday morning, she went to the interview, took the test, and I was on the road taking her back home Saturday morning. Monday morning, shortly after I arrived back in Wilmore, she called and told me they had offered her the job; she accepted and two weeks later, she had resigned her job, packed up, and moved all of our furniture and belongings to the attic, turned our house over to our daughter and her new husband and moved in with me. We later decided to sell our home to our daughter and her husband.

I know without a doubt that God had a hand in the way things turned out for us. There were too many doors opening and too many opportunities that fit our situation for them to be coincidences.

Seminary life was a whole lot better now that Gloria and I were together. My trips back and forth to Detroit to fulfill my obligation to preach on the weekends became more relaxing and less stressful with Gloria riding with me.

When I traveled alone, I would try and make the trip in record time; I hardly ever stopped to rest or get something to eat. One Sunday, I made the 400-mile trip in less than five hours. But that all changed when Gloria was with me. My trips went from five and a half hours to six and a half to seven hours. At first I complained, but after a while I started to see the advantages of taking time to rest; and to stretch my legs during the trip. Plus, it was good to have someone to talk with while I sitting in the many traffic jams that we ran into on I-75.

I have always had difficulty when it comes to learning from books and listening to lectures. However, if I were to witness a task being done, I could duplicate the process easily. I could not understand why it was so difficult for me to remember a page from a book thirty seconds after I read it. I could sit through a lecture, listening intently to the professor; and when he was done, I could not remember a third of what he had lectured on. The notes I took were useless when it came to studying for an exam; I felt like I was wasting my time.

In the first summer after enrolling in seminary, I signed up for an accelerated class in the Greek language. It was a course that lasted eight weeks instead of the usual sixteen weeks. I studied around the clock relying on memorization a great deal. I simply could not retain the process for working the formulas. Every moment I was not in class, I used for studying; I hardly took time out to eat or sleep. By the end of the class, my hard work and perseverance paid off; I succeeded in passing the class with a grade of 88, which was the lowest grade I could get and still pass. Only one other person got a grade lower than me (but he hardly ever attended class). Ninety-eight percent of the class got grades between 98 and 100.

During the regular semesters, I was also struggling in all my other classes as well. I worked and studied hard, but most of the time, I was lost. This went on for almost two years of my seminary education. Early in my fourth semester, I went to one of my professors after class and told her I was "not getting it." I explained to her that the information made sense while she was presenting it, but I was finding it hard to retain what I was hearing and reading.

After talking with her, she suggested I go and talk with another professor who was very good at discerning learning disabilities. I made an appointment to see the other professor; after putting me through a series of tests, he referred me to a specialist who lived about a hundred miles north of the seminary.

I immediately called her and made an appointment to see her. When I got there, she had me do a battery of exercises, both visual and audio. Then she sat me down, asking me the same question I had been asking myself. "Why are you in graduate school?" She said to me, "People like you don't usually graduate from high school." She was right; if you remember, I quit when I turned sixteen years of age.

She went on to explain that I was borderline dyslexic who also had a condition known as Adult Attention Deficit Disorder. Just when I thought I had heard the worst, she told me that I have what is known as Abnormal Dominus.

This is a rare condition only found in young males. The best definition I can give is that I am left-handed but right-side dominant. Instead of being right- or left-brain dominant, both sides of my brain try to work at the same time. She said it was a condition that made learning very difficult; but there were exercises that I could do to help me to understand and comprehend things a little better. This condition usually leaves you confused and frustrated when trying to grasp something new.

The way she explained it to me was that I receive and process information differently than normal people; when you add the dyslexia and attention deficit disorder to the mix, it makes learning very difficult.

She also went on to tell me that people with these kinds of learning disabilities were usually very creative. (Boy, did she hit that one on the head!)

She was right. I find ways to get things done that most people would never even think about. For instance, I used to read my books looking for the answer to the questions I knew would be on the test, underline and memorize what I needed to know, then move on to the next question. Early the next day, I would go back, read, and reread just the part I needed to know for the test. There were other little tricks I used to help me get through the next two and a half years, and allow me to graduate with a 3.7 GPA. I was getting the right answers, but I wasn't learning anything.

I continued to visit the learning specialist for about two months. She taught me different ways to overcome some of my anxiety toward learning. To be honest, I thought I was just plain dumb. But she assured me I was not dumb, only that the way I processed information was not normal. She promised me that if I did the little exercises she prescribed for me, I would see a noticeable difference in my ability to read and retain data.

When I can read (and listen to what I am reading) at the same time, it really seems to help. I began to read out loud so I could hear the words as I read. This made a big difference; I could focus on what I was reading for a longer period. Usually, if I read silently, I could go through two or three pages and not remember a thing I had read.

It was a good feeling to finally learn that my problem with learning was not because I was dumb, but because I had learning disabilities that should have been addressed early in life; normally, while I was in grade school or junior high. Instead, I had just turned fifty-seven years old when this was brought to my attention.

I thank God every day for the professor who took the time to listen to me, took the time to investigate, and help me get some help.

At the end of my second year of seminary, the deadline for paying my tuition was two days away. The grant I was counting on fell through, and I was about to be booted out of school because you could not sign up for the next semester until you had paid for the previous one. I thought I was off the hook with my commitment to God. If I didn't have the money, then I would have to drop out and move back home.

The day before the deadline, I was walking down the hall on the way to the chapel when one of the admissions counselors, who worked in the office with Gloria, came running out the door when she saw me. She asked if I had talked to Gloria. I told her not since she left for work. The counselor took me by the arm and said, "Come with me!" as she almost dragged me into the Admissions Office.

We went into the back entrance of the Admissions Office and she took me up to Gloria's desk. Gloria asked if I had spoken with Mary (the director in the Finance Office.), I said, "No, I had not," and asked, "Why?"

That's when I knew that God was not going to let me weasel out of my commitment. Gloria told me Mary had called and told her that an anonymous donor had just deposited four thousand dollars into my student account. Before that anonymous gift, I was short $3998.00. Now, I had a two-dollar surplus in my account and could register for the next semester's classes. This anonymous donor did this two more times before I graduated.

By this time, I had made it through two years and I only had a year to go, if I could continue taking classes all year long without taking any time off.

But it was not to be. In the fall of 2000, I developed a serious case of pneumonia and had to sit out a winter semester, which threw me off my three-year plan.

Return to Michigan

Many things happened to make my last year at seminary a cakewalk. For one, I had completed all my mandatory classes, so all I had to take were electives. I chose classes that required little or no homework and classes I enjoyed, like photography, web design, and storytelling.

God really blessed me when my supervising pastor (from Michigan) brought the youth from my home church down to an Ichthus concert for the weekend.

The Sunday morning before they went back to Michigan, I took my supervisor and the youth to attend church services at the church where I was volunteering as a student pastor. As we were sitting there in service, my supervisor leaned over and said to me, "You don't have to preach the evening service anymore; you can preach in the morning worship from now on." So for the rest of my seminary time, she allowed me to preach the morning service, which meant Gloria and I could be on the road back to Kentucky by one or two in the afternoon.

I guess after making the drive down herself, my supervising pastor realized what it must have been like for me to do it late at night every week.

The year went fast and, in no time at all, graduation day was only a few weeks away. This in itself created a dilemma. On the weekend of my seminary graduation, I had to drive to Adrian, Michigan, to appear before the annual conference on Saturday. Immediately following my appearance before the conference, I drove back to Kentucky to prepare for graduation day ceremonies, which were on Sunday afternoon. After graduation that Sunday night, Gloria and I were on our way back to Michigan for my ordination as a probationary elder into the United Methodist Church, which was held on Monday afternoon. After my ordination ceremony and a celebration dinner, we spent the night in Michigan, got up Tuesday morning, and drove back to Kentucky to pack and move out of our seminary apartment.

I thank God for the many friends who came by to help us pack and load the rental truck. After thoroughly cleaning the apartment, we turned in the keys and headed to Westland, Michigan, where we would stay for two years before I would be transferred to a church in Flint, Michigan.

Back in Michigan, I served at the Cass Community UMC for two more years. In 2003, I asked to be transferred to a new church. From July 1997 until June 2003, I was working as the supervising pastor under the direction of the senior pastor. When I first returned home, things were going well; we worked well together. But somewhere in the course of two years, our personalities began to get in the way and I asked to be transferred. I will be the first to admit that the differences that came between us were all my fault.

I owe much gratitude to my supervisor. First, for allowing me to stay on while attending seminary, and secondly, for what I learned about serving others while working with her. She was always there for me when I needed her, and she always treated me with respect. I felt guilty after I left. There have been many times when I have regretted my decision to leave.

When I arrived at my new charge in Flint, Michigan, I tried to put some of the things I had learned from her into practice. I learned quickly that there was a lot more to being the senior pastor than I realized.

My first goals were to get several of the programs I wanted to start off the ground. None of the programs took root; all failed.

It had looked easy the way she did it. I came to realize that it takes more than good intentions to do what she was doing. It takes a special calling from God and genuine love and compassion for the people you have been called to serve. She had it!—and I didn't, at the time.

Secondly, sometimes you had to be able to make tough decisions, many of which people sometimes might not agree with; but, nevertheless, you have to make them if you want to be successful in what you're trying to accomplish.

I am grateful for my years of working with her, because now I understand how she was able to start and run the many caring ministry programs, many of which (if not all) are in operation today, for the people in the Cass Corridor and beyond. But more importantly, I understand that many of the things she did, which I disagreed with then, were necessary.

In July 2003, I was assigned to Flint Trinity UMC as the senior pastor. It would take four years of hard work before I realized that the church just did not want to grow. The people were comfortable coming to worship every Sunday morning, then spending an hour in the fellowship hall catching up with old friends.

In years past, Flint Trinity United Methodist Church was a vibrant and healthy community of believers, very active in ministry, who did a lot for the surrounding community. But after the automobile factories closed or moved away, the neighborhood underwent a major change in population. Many of the middle-class families began to move away to the suburbs. They were replaced by low-income families who were looking to own their own home, but didn't realize the cost and expense of maintenance on their properties.

Today, these once beautiful homes around the church, and in the surrounding communities, are no longer nice-looking, nor well-maintained. The neighborhood has more abandoned homes than it does occupied ones. Crime, drug trafficking, and prostitution have made it unsafe and dangerous to walk the streets, even in the daylight hours.

The members who were still coming to worship at the church were driving in from the suburbs. The majority of them were white, elderly couples who had moved away several years before, but didn't want to give up on their church.

When I arrived to take over as the new pastor, the church was down to about fifty active members who were just trying to hang on and keep the doors open. We tried to reach out to the people in the community, but it was no use. Those members who could do something, didn't because they felt it wasn't safe, while the others only came into town on Sunday.

I didn't want to request a new assignment, but Gloria was starting to feel unsafe, and I didn't like to leave her at home when I had to go away. Burglars breaking into occupied homes in that community was as common as breathing. It happened at night and in broad daylight while neighbors were watching.

After coming home one day to find a guy standing in my garage (which was locked when I left home), I called the district superintendent and told him we wanted out.

When I told the administrative board about my decision, the members voted unanimously to close the doors. Most of them were driving in from the suburbs to the inner city where the church was located, while the area was getting worse by the day. They told the district superintendent that they did not want a new pastor and that they were going to find a church closer to where they lived. At the time of closing, the church was down to about thirty active members or fewer, which was down from twelve hundred at its peak in the 60s and 70s.

On June 30, 2007, the doors of Trinity United Methodist Church closed for the last time, and Gloria and I moved on to our new assignment.

While waiting for the district superintendent to get back with us, we tried to think of a church where we might possibly be sent, and we could only come up with two—both of them in Detroit.

Fowlerville

One night around ten o'clock, the phone rang. The caller ID indicated it was a 734 area code. When I answered, the person on the other end of the line was the Ann Arbor district superintendent. He was calling to inform me that the cabinet had come up with a church where they thought I would be a good fit. Before he told me the name of the church, he started to detail all the qualities and gifts the people were looking for in a pastor. He thought this assignment would be perfect for me.

Meanwhile, I'm still trying to figure out the name of the church. Finally, he told me. He said, "The church is in Fowlerville."

My first thought was, *You've got to be kidding me!* I said, "Fowlerville?" adding, "Do you know who you're talking to? This is Tom Tarpley."

"I know," he replied, "and we want you to go to Fowlerville."

Based on everything I had heard about Fowlerville and the Howell area, I was ready to tell him, "No thanks; if that is all you have, then I'll retire." Instead, I told him I needed time to pray about it; which Gloria and I both did.

One of the first things I did was to get on the internet and Google, Fowlerville demographics. I found out that the population was ninety-six percent white, two percent Spanish, one percent black, and one percent other. I then called the president of the Diversity Council in Livingston County and talked with her. She assured me that the reputation on the outside was nothing like it was in the community. That was good to hear.

I then started to read as much as I could find on the area. Believe me, some of it was not very comforting or assuring given my situation. Despite all that, a few days later, I called the district superintendent, and accepted the offer to go to Fowlerville to become the pastor of the First United Methodist Church. It was the best thing to happen to me since I married my Gloria.

(Moving from Flint to Fowlerville was like going from hell to paradise.) The first day after our arrival, Gloria and I woke up to a beautiful sunshiny day with two of the prettiest deer we've ever seen standing in our backyard. Our new neighbors came over to welcome us, and everyone we ran into made us feel welcome.

The few remaining members in our Flint congregation had concerns about our safety as well, so when I stepped into the pulpit that first Sunday, more than half of them had driven over fifty miles to be in worship in our new church and offer us their support. They were pleased with the reception we received, and we all went out to lunch after the service.

We were privileged to serve eight years at the Fowlerville United Methodist Church. We have enjoyed serving in Fowlerville more than any other place we have been.

In my years of living, I have made some poor judgments and some bad decisions, but moving to Fowlerville was not among them. My time in Fowlerville, as Pastor of the UMC, has been nothing but rewarding. From the first day—till I retired in June 2015, Gloria and I enjoyed our time in Fowlerville.

We've enjoyed it so much that after our retirement, we bought a condominium in the village so that we could stay in the community we had come to love.

Gloria

"The greatest thing you'll ever learn is to love and be loved in return" (*Nat King Cole, Nature Boy*).

Those lyrics of the old song sung by Nat King Cole sum up my life. My most treasured desire in life was for someone to love, and to have them love me in return; but I never realized the true meaning of love until I met my present wife, Gloria, who has been by my side for more than forty-three years. She has stuck by me when I was at my lowest, and my highest. She has always been there for me, no matter what I was going through. Gloria's love helped to get me through many trials (which I may have failed) if not for her support.

When we met, I had only been living in Detroit for less than a year. Gloria came to view an apartment in the complex where I worked. She liked the apartment I showed her and she took possession of it a few weeks later. After moving in, I didn't take an interest in her mainly because I was seeing two other women who lived in her building.

Besides that, she was short and I didn't particularly care for short women. However, I did noticed that she had a good figure.

At the time, I was married; but my marriage was not very healthy. My wife used to leave me, then run back to Pontiac every time she got angry at me—which was often. Most weekends, I was free to do what I wanted because she was out of town visiting her sisters. This was fine with me because I enjoyed the freedom to hang out and party with my supervisor and other friends in the apartment complex.

Gloria had been living in the complex for almost two years before the opportunity presented itself for me to ask her out.

I remember one night, I had been upstairs in the apartment over hers visiting one of the ladies I was seeing, and I was quietly making my exit from upstairs (in an attempt to sneak out the back door of her building without being seen). Just as I was in front of her door, it opened, and she saw me. I spoke and continued to exit the building. Later, after we started dating, she told me she used to see me coming from upstairs all the time.

In those days, I was known as the "backdoor bandit." (Not something I'm proud of today, but it was who I was). I would sneak around to different apartments by going in the back entrance where hopefully no one would see me.

In 1973, my ex-wife moved out and left me for good. She took my daughter with her and the two of them got an apartment in Pontiac. What I didn't know was that she was also having an affair with one of the part-time workers that I hired to work for me at the complex. He had been trying to get her to leave me and she finally took him up on his offer. I learned that shortly after she moved out and the two of them started living together.

At first I was angry but after thinking about it, I realized it was the best thing that could have happened to me. At last I was free with no one to answer to but myself. It was a good time in my life. But, eventually, I started to miss having someone around when I got home at night.

I made frequent trips out to Pontiac on the weekend to get my daughter and the two of us would hang out. During this time, when I was drinking and getting high all the time; usually my daughter was with me.

One day, I needed to send some money to a friend in California. I knew that Gloria worked for Western Union, so I went over to her apartment to see if she could help me.

While I was there, I decided to ask her out. She accepted, and slowly we started to see each other on a regular basis. At first, I was still trying to maintain my harem; but slowly, one by one, I stopped seeing the rest of the ladies I was dating.

Gloria became my one and only girlfriend.

One night, I received a call from Child Protective Services (CPS). They called to inform me that they had my ten-year-old son in lockup. The police had picked him up walking the street about two or three in the morning.

Meanwhile, I talked to my daughter's mother into giving me full custody of our daughter. Now, I found myself living with a four-year-old daughter and a twelve-year-old son.

I thank God for Gloria because she stepped in and took care of my children while I was getting drunk and high on drugs and hanging out with my friends. She had a great relationship with both kids, and she treated them as though they were her very own.

My wife finally filed for divorce, and in November of 1974, I became a single man. This was great but it wouldn't last very long. In the summer of 1975, I asked Gloria to marry me and she accepted. In September of the same year, we were married in a small ceremony at the home of my aunt (mother's sister), with both of our families and a few friends in attendance.

A couple of years after Gloria and I were married, my children started to act up and decided that they would rather live with their mothers, where they could have more freedom. I gave them a few months to think it over before allowing them to go. But after a while, I consented and they moved back to their mother's home.

Getting married didn't bring on a lot of change in me. Instead of slowing down, my night-life activities increased. During that entire time, Gloria hardly ever complained about what I was doing, even when she would get home from work and find the house full of people getting high.

I took pride in my drugs, and I always had the best that could be found, regardless of what it cost. The reason people liked to hang out at my place was because I kept my bar stocked with the finest liquor and wine and everything was free. I loved being told how good the dope was at my place. Sometimes, I would spend the whole day in the den entertaining and getting high with whoever stopped by. It was no different from my early years when I would buy friends with candy and cigarettes. After the drugs and liquor were gone, so were the so called friends.

As the years went by, I became more difficult to live with, but Gloria simply ignored me; which made me angry. I wanted to argue with her, so that she would make me mad. Then I would tell her to leave. I would come in drunk and verbally abuse her, and, sometimes, I was so harsh until I made her cry. However, she would not argue with me, no matter what I did or said. She would instead go into the bedroom, close the door, and start watching TV.

To this day, I do not know why she stayed with me. Yet she did, and I thank God every day for her presence in my life. She was "the rock" that kept me anchored until God had a chance to turn me around. She was exactly what I needed, and I owe her more than I can ever repay. She kept me from making some mistakes that could have cost me my life, or possibly have sent me to prison for a very long time.

At one point, when we were not getting along, we attended a post-marital counseling session at our church. Our pastor explained something to me that made me understand why Gloria was so good for me. He said with my mood swings, I was like a bouncing ball, up and down, up and down, up and down; and Gloria was steady—like a flat line on a heart monitor after a person's heart has stopped.

"Because of Gloria's level-headedness and her ability to remain the same, she took some of the highs out of my 'high' and the lows out of my 'lows,' which made me more steady, and less like a jumping jack," he explained.

For many years, I tried to change her, wanting her to be more like me. However, she is as solid as a rock when it comes to doing what is right and maintaining a sense of integrity. Over the years. she has rubbed off on me more than I have on her, which is a very good thing.

Bringing it Home

As I look back, reflecting on the many years of loneliness and unhappiness of my life, I realize how so much of my unhappiness came from my desire to be loved and accepted. As far back as I can remember, I have tried to be a people pleaser, always doing what I thought others wanted me to do, rather than following my own mind and instincts. I would go out of my way to make people like me. This desire to be accepted, allowed others to use and manipulate me into doing a lot of crazy things that I would never have done had I not been so desperate to find acceptance.

After many years of being used, I learned how to use the same manipulative tools on others to get almost anything I wanted. I could sweet talk and charm almost anyone to get what I wanted.

I can remember that during my pre-teen years, my brother Aaron was always my mother's favorite. She allowed him to get away with just about anything, whereas I got scolded for almost everything I did.

Sometimes, I would hang around the house and do housework, or whatever I could, to try and get my mother to show me the same kind of love she lavished on him. This affection for me would only come after he was killed in a car crash in 1979. After his death, I became the oldest child and mom began to treat me the way she did him.

I can't remember if there was ever a time when I didn't feel insecure and out of place. I thought all the kids in the neighborhood were better than me. I was not very good at anything I tried.

Most of my time was spent standing around, watching the other boys participate in sports, dancing, and having a great time; while I only dreamed of being able to do what they did. My teenage and young adult years were some of the saddest years of my life. The many years of verbal abuse had taken away my self-esteem; and I felt inferior to almost everyone around me. I know now, that I drank a lot of alcohol because it was the only way I could ease the pain of my feelings of not being wanted.

Life's Continuous Struggle

I have shared with you what my former life was like, including some of the events that happened during my early childhood (that I now feel were responsible for making me the kind of person I became later in life.) Now I will share about the person I am today.

Today, I know that everything that took place in my early life was preparing me for the task that God had for me to do today. All the trials and tribulations I faced have made me a more compassionate and empathetic person when it comes to people struggling with unnecessary baggage. Whereas I used to be extremely judgmental and very critical of people who do wrong, today, I take into consideration that I don't know what kind of past experiences a person may have endured that makes them act the way they do.

This change in my attitude and behavior was not sudden; it has gradually changed over the years as I have worked on building my relationship with Jesus Christ. The closer I get in my walk with Christ, the more I see that

God loves the sinner just as much as he loves his faithful followers. God doesn't want any of his children to miss out on heaven. He proved that when he sent his Son Jesus to die on the cross for all of us.

But, I must say in all honesty, I have much difficulty in living the way I know I should. I am reminded of a passage of Scripture from the book of Romans that the Apostle Paul wrote about his struggle with obeying God. It can be found in Romans, chapter seven, verses fourteen to twenty-five. It is copied below.

"We know that the Law is right and good, but I am a person who does what is wrong and bad. I am not my own boss. Sin is my boss. I do not understand myself. I want to do what is right but I do not do it. Instead, I do the very thing I hate. When I do the thing I do not want to do, it shows me that the Law is right and good.

"So I am not doing it. Sin living in me is doing it. I know there is nothing good in me, that is, in my flesh. For I want to do good but I do not. I do not do the good I want to do. Instead, I am always doing the sinful things I do not want to do. If I am always doing the very thing I do not want to do, it means I am no longer the one who does it. It is sin that lives in me. This has become my way of life: When I want to do what is right, I always do what is wrong. My mind and heart agree with the Law of God. But there is a different law at work deep

inside of me that fights with my mind. This law of sin holds me in its power because sin is still in me.

"There is no happiness in me! Who can set me free from my sinful old self? God's Law has power over my mind, but sin still has power over my sinful old self. I thank God I can be free through Jesus Christ our Lord!" (Rom. 7:14–25, NLT).

I have always wanted to do what is right. But just as the Apostle Paul writes in the Scripture above, I have made some bad choices during my lifetime.

I knew I was doing wrong when I lied, stole, abused drugs and alcohol, and committed other sins, but the temptation to give in to the desires of my fleshly nature always seemed to win the battle raging in me between good and evil.

Many nights were spent with me sitting in the dark beating myself up because of some evil deed I committed against God or another human being. When it came to making choices, I always knew beforehand what was the right choice; but I usually found myself doing exactly the opposite of what I knew was right.

The battle between making wise choices or bad choices still rages on every day deep within me. What makes the difference today is my relationship with Jesus Christ. Unlike before, I came to know Christ, my desire today is to please Him. Therefore, when faced with some temptation to do the wrong thing, I turn to Jesus and ask for His help to resist the schemes of the enemy, which only wants to draw me away from following Christ.

The road that leads to "hell" is paved with "good intentions." It is a very wide road and very easy to follow because it is the road most traveled. There are no obstacles along the way and the journey is all downhill. It doesn't take a lot of effort to travel this road.

But beware, everyone who chooses this road will one day stand before the Creator for judgment and his verdict will not be in their favor.

On the other hand, there is another road that is much narrower. It is not as easy to maneuver as the wide road because it is the road that leads us to Christ.

The enemy of Christ, the devil, using his three most effective weapons, mainly the lust of the flesh, the lust of the eye, and the pride of life, has created many diversions along this narrow road, because he wants to distract us, drawing our attention away from seeking after God.

Jesus says in Matthew 26:41, "Watch and pray so that you will not fall into temptation. The spirit is willing, but the flesh is weak."

The devil is no fool; he knows this. That is why all his diversion tactics are aimed at the flesh.

The journey down the wide road will be more pleasant and enjoyable, but when you reach your destination, "there

THOMAS E. TARPLEY SR.

will be weeping and gnashing of teeth, for you will see Abraham, Isaac, Jacob, and all the prophets in the Kingdom of God, but you will be thrown out" (Luke 13:28, NLT).

It is unfortunate, but very few people will find the narrow road because they are too caught up in following and seeking to satisfy the cravings of their sinful nature.

Jesus said: "The gateway to life is very narrow and the road is difficult, and only a few ever find it" (Matt. 7:14, NLT).

When John the Baptist was preaching in the wilderness, he was preparing the way for the coming Messiah. John did what those of us who are sincere followers of Christ are doing today. We need to be encouraging people to repent and turn back to Christ; and we should not go about it as if we are afraid or ashamed. We should be shouting it out for all the world to hear, both in our words and in our lifestyles.

I am a grateful believer in Jesus Christ, and I preach the Gospel of Christ and his resurrection. I am not ashamed of the Gospel; I will preach it until God calls me home.

Yes! I still struggle with the sinful nature that lives within me, but unlike in my earlier years, I don't have to struggle alone. I now have the power of the Holy Spirit, which gives me the power to resist those sinful temptations. I can now claim victory because Jesus overcame the power of sin and death.

We all died with Jesus on the cross; we all rose again with him on that Easter morning when he stepped out of his tomb symbolizing that the victory belongs to the Lord.

To win the war between the flesh and the Spirit, we must be connected to the power of God that comes from being in a close and personal relationship with him.

Never allow what others say about you define who you are. I bought into what people were saying about me, and it almost ruined my life. I was ashamed of who I was and afraid to do anything about it. The ridicule and unkind words that appeared to be aimed at me festered inside me like a cancerous sore eating away my self-esteem, my confidence in myself, and my joy for living.

When I stopped listening to others and began believing in myself, I was gradually able to let go of the hurts, habits, and behavior traits of the past. I began to see that I was better than what people were saying about me. Now I know that I am exactly who God wants me to be; doing exactly what he wants me to do in the place where he has placed me. And for that I am grateful and joyously proud.

I can't go back and change the past nor do I want to. What I can do is share my experiences in life with others with the hope of helping them to see that they do not have to go through what I went through.

One of the last battles I have been fighting came to an end when I got baptized in the spring of 2017. For many years, I had been wrestling with the idea that I needed to be baptized. I knew I had been baptized as a child, but that was before I knew anything about God or what it meant to be baptized. The thought of getting up in front of a crowd terrified me and I kept putting it off. After all, what would people think? What would they say? I was a pastor, and for me to get up and confess that I felt the need to be baptized at my age, didn't play to well in my mind. I am grateful to have a pastor who believes in teaching as well as preaching. His sermons have inspired me to dig deeper and to step out in faith in many area of my life and ministry.

Fear (false evidence appearing as real) drove me into the gutter where I wallowed in sin for almost five decades. But grace set me free to be the person God wanted me to be.

About the Author

 Thomas lived in a world of fear, created by low self-esteem and a poor self-image, for more than forty years. To cope with this fear, he turned to alcohol and later in life, as he grew into a young man, he added drugs to the mix. His life had no purpose, except to get as high as he could, for a long as he could as often as he could. After one failed serious relationship and one failed marriage, he remarried in 1975 and his life began to slowly change, and he found himself going back to church after being away for almost twenty-five years.

Late in life, at the age of fifty-five, he felt the call of God on his life. He walked away from a lucrative career as an independent sales representative and enrolled in Cleary College, seeking to obtain an undergrad degree, before going on to attend Asbury Theological Seminary, where he earned a master's degree in divinity. Thomas was forced to retire in 2015 because of the mandatory retirement law in the United Methodist church.

Thomas and his wife, Gloria, of forty-two years now live in Fowlerville, Michigan, where they are both very active in spreading the gospel. Although retired from the United Methodist church, Thomas serves as the care pastor at the Fowlerville, UB church near their home. He is also the ministry leader of the Fowlerville UB Celebrate Recovery program, a Christian-based program that helps people work through their hurts, habits, and hang-ups.

CPSIA information can be obtained
at www.ICGtesting.com
Printed in the USA
FFOW05n0854110917

9 781640 799646